50 Democracy Ideas
You Really
Need to Know

Adam Fleming

greenfinch

Contents

Introduction

Attending a reception to mark the tenth anniversary of the introduction of same sex marriage in the United Kingdom, the part I enjoyed most was a discussion among some of those involved about how this historic change had happened, and without anyone voting for it, either in an election or a referendum.

In a video, former Prime Minister David Cameron, a Conservative, explained that his wife had softened his traditionalist views and he thanked his political opponents for helping to build a consensus. A former junior minister, a Liberal Democrat, recalled being advised to conquer the drudgery of governing by focusing on one policy that could stand the test of time; equal marriage had been hers. A legendary activist explained that his target had been a court ruling from 1971 that interpreted existing marriage laws in a restrictive way. A publisher told of pre-recording supportive video messages from celebrities and citizens so that whenever a negative news story dropped, there was a positive version. Another campaigner explained how Britain's incomplete separation of church and state meant Parliament could only mandate so much when it came to religion.

During the discussion I mentally ticked off many of the topics in this book – government, legislatures, church and state, influence, the courts, the media, the constitution, liberal democracy, representative democracy, majoritarian democracy, politicians, leaders, even a bit of federalism – things that prove 'democracy' is about a lot more than just the act of voting or whatever politics is happening that day.

I have spent much of my life reporting on the latter without much time to think about the big theories driving events, and this is my attempt to address that. Rather than try to replicate the many good encyclopedias out there, I offer a series of chapters to provide a readable overview from which you can come to your own conclusions, rather than hearing mine. Democracy is both older and newer than you might think. How it works in other places can feel simultaneously familiar and very different. And to quote the politician that I have reported on the most – the EU's chief Brexit negotiator Michel Barnier – 'It's an ongoing process'.

Adam Fleming

01 Ancient Democracies

When the academic Jean-Paul Gagnon carried out a search to find how many different versions of democracy featured in literature, the media and on the internet, he discovered . . . 2,234 of them. The word originated in Greece in around 500 BCE – or more specifically, Athens, a dominant city-state among a collection of settlements rather than a coherent country. In Greek, *demos* means 'people', and *kratos*, 'power'. People power.

The oldest-surviving sales pitch for the Athenian model of democracy comes from a speech given in 431 BCE by the city's ruler Pericles. The historian Thucydides wrote it down several decades later. Pericles was delivering the eulogy at the annual mass public funeral for the victims of the ongoing Peloponnesian War. 'It is true that we are called a democracy, for the administration is in the hands of the many and not of the few,' he said. With the bones of the dead laid out in a tent nearby, he explained:

> 'Here each individual is interested not only in his own affairs but in the affairs of the state as well: even those who are mostly occupied with their own business are extremely well informed on general politics – this is a peculiarity of ours: we do not say that a man who takes no interest in politics is a man who minds his own business; we say that he has no business here at all.'

Elements of Athenian democracy

The main peculiarity of Athenian democracy to modern eyes is how hands-on it was compared to a 21st-century representative democracy. Forty times a year, at least 6,000 ordinary citizens – although not really all citizens, only men over 20 who had completed two years of military service – would meet at the *ecclesia*, or assembly. Orators would make their case in policy areas from taxation to the navy. Proceedings were underpinned by *parrhesia* – freedom of speech – and *isegoria* – the right of equal participation for all. The aim was for decisions to be unanimous, but disagreements would be settled by a show of hands.

These sessions took place at the Pnyx, an amphitheatre carved into the hillside. Its design evolved over time, but in one iteration speakers stood on a stage called the *bema* with only the sky behind them. They faced the sun for most of the day so there would be no shadows on their faces, and the reactions of the assembled citizenry would be visible to all. It was designed to provide maximum clarity.

The work of the assembly was managed by the *boule*. This was also known as the Council of 500 because each of the city's ten tribes sent fifty members, who could be farmers, sailors, businesspeople, teachers, anyone. The president of the *boule*'s term lasted a single day. A group of council members was on standby every hour of every day to handle urgent matters. There was a mixture of courts, where criminal cases were heard and where laws were assessed.

Random chance was an important element of Athenian democracy. Selection for membership of the *boule*, for juries and for many roles in Athenian officialdom, such as tax collection, was done by lot, a process known as sortition. That anyone could serve helped to conjure a sense of political equality in the city. It also meant there was less need for elections, and the rivalries that came with them. Selecting individuals randomly rather than on merit, served as a check on their egos. The ever-revolving cast in officialdom also meant that the assembly remained as a powerful constant. A benign interpretation is that it reinforced the primacy of this most democratic body; a more cynical view holds that it maintained the power of individuals who knew how to manipulate the assembled mass.

The constitution

All of this is known thanks to fragments of speeches, archaeological evidence and reports by ancient historians. The clearest account comes from Aristotle in his *Athenian Constitution*, discovered on papyrus scrolls in Egypt in the late 19th century. The work splits in two – a history of the development of the Athenian state followed by a detailed rundown of how it worked – and it feels as detailed as the rules of procedure found on any parliamentary website today. There are two problems, though. Firstly, a leading Aristotelian scholar said the history section is 'mostly rubbish', and, secondly, it was probably not written by Aristotle but by his pupils, and only attributed to him for branding purposes.

At around the same time as the move towards democracy in ancient Greece, the ancient Romans were establishing another governing model – the republic. *Res* meant 'affair' in Latin, and *publicus*, 'people'. In its most basic form republicanism meant rejection of rule by the king, and a partnership between the people and the ruling elite of the Senate. This relationship was visible everywhere in the stamp that adorned money, official documents, public buildings and soliders' banners: SPQR – *Senatus Populusque Romanus* – The Senate and the People of Rome. Cicero summed it up: 'While power resides in the people, authority rests with the Senate.'

There were democratic elements. Every year, the people elected two senators to serve as consuls. They commanded the army, chaired the Senate and alternated duties on a monthly basis. There was an assembly, entry to which was granted by Roman citizenship, which applied very widely. But as the empire expanded geographically, fewer citizens were able to attend. Around 50 influential families, called *gentes*, wielded power. The consuls and the assembly became weaker as the Roman emperors grew stronger.

The cradle of democracy

Ancient Athens and Rome have dominated the history of democracy because accounts of them have survived and because much of the history has been written from a Western perspective. These ancient models have had longevity, quoted from the days of St Thomas Aquinas in the 13th century to the Occupy Wall Street protestors in the 21st. But archaeologists have uncovered evidence of assembly-style bodies existing much earlier and much further east than Greece. Historians point out that Confucius was writing about the nature of government in China before Plato was born, while the philosopher Chanakya was theorizing about power and accountability in India shortly after the death of Aristotle.

The rose-tinted idea of Athens as the 'cradle of democracy' has been revised, too, with scholars highlighting a number of problems. Namely, that the city was not really that democratic because its version of democracy excluded women, immigrants and slaves. Slaves outnumbered the free in Athens by three to two, according to some estimates. And an 'immigrant' could be someone whose family had lived there for some time. The apparently level playing field of the assembly has also been described as an illusion because it could be dominated by those who had the time, money and training to sway the crowd. Even Pericles' famous homage to the Athenian system has been questioned – was it just fighting talk to keep the population motivated in the war against Sparta? Or maybe it was only quoted to serve as a warning to future generations about how easily the mob could be stirred?

The condensed idea
In the hands of the many not the few

02 Political Animals

Two millennia ago, Aristotle wrote: 'Man is by nature a political animal.' By this he meant that human beings inevitably form attachments – families and communities – that gradually develop into villages that then turn into towns, which become cities. This, Aristotle believed, is because 'Every man has by nature an impulse toward a partnership with others'. The insights that flowed from this, particularly in Aristotle's monumental work *The Politics*, have left most political thinkers indebted to him. Aristotle was not just a tutor to a young Alexander the Great . . . but to everyone.

Who rules?

After looking at the multiple types of constitutional arrangement he saw around him, Aristotle asked himself: 'Who rules and on whose behalf?' The philosopher developed three types of constitution – rule by the one, by the few or by the many. Each version could be done well or selfishly. Rule by one was monarchy, and its evil twin was tyranny. Leadership by the few was aristocracy, and its perverted form,

The *polis*

Aristotle gave the name *polis* to a city in which people cooperated in its administration for their mutual benefit. The *polis* was a place where man could seek the good life, and his pursuit of the virtues of kindness and beauty should be enabled by the rulers of the city. All of this was perfectly natural, Aristotle thought. He also wrote extensively on justice and equality – although this equality did not extend to slaves or people who were not deemed intelligent enough to participate in public life. And while he believed that women had the ability to think for themselves, he also determined that they needed the 'supervision' of men.

oligarchy. The ideal form was 'polity', which was a sweet spot where smart, ethical citizens collaborated in the common interest. The suboptimal version of polity tended to be unstable because it incorporated the rowdy and uninformed poor. Aristotle called this . . . democracy. He concluded:

'. . . constitutions that aim at the common advantage are correct and just without qualification, whereas those that aim only at the advantage of the rulers are deviant and unjust, because they involve despotic rule, which is inappropriate for a community of free persons.'

Aristotle believed that the ideal constitution was probably a mixture of all of them, and that democracy was the best option if a five-star-quality polity could not be constructed.

Plato

On the other hand, Plato, Aristotle's elder, had little time for the concept of democracy. He had reason to be cynical of popular power because the citizens in the assembly had just sentenced his mentor Socrates to death (the philosopher beat them to it by drinking poison). Athens had also been defeated by Sparta, so its model did not look strong. Plato's critique of Athenian democracy is found in his epic meditation on the ideal state, *The Republic*. At one point he talked about someone looking after 'a large and powerful animal' (read: the public). The keeper might know a lot about the animal's diet and how generally to keep it under control, but if it is to be properly cared for or nurtured, Plato said, the keeper should really know what it finds 'admirable or shameful, good or bad, right or wrong'. This was about the difficulty of really knowing the public will, and a warning about the dangers of populism and of demagoguery.

Another of Plato's metaphors lies in an extended anecdote about an imaginary ship on a troubled voyage with an argumentative crew and a captain who is a bit deaf and partially sighted:

'The crew are all quarrelling with each other about how to navigate the ship, each thinking he ought to be at the helm; they have never learned the art of navigation and cannot say that anyone ever taught it them, or that they spent any time studying it; indeed they say it can't be taught and are ready to murder anyone who says it can. They spend all their time milling round the captain and doing all they can to get him to give them the helm. If one faction is more successful than another, their rivals may kill them and throw them overboard, lay out the honest captain with drugs or drink or in some other way, take control of the ship, help themselves to what's on board, and turn the voyage into the sort of drunken pleasure-cruise you would expect. Finally, they reserve their admiration for the man who knows how to lend a hand in controlling the captain by force or fraud; they praise his seamanship and navigation and knowledge of the sea and condemn everyone else as useless. They have no idea that the true navigator must study the seasons of the year, the sky, the stars, the winds and all the other subjects appropriate to his profession . . . With all this going on aboard, aren't the sailors on any such ship bound to regard the true navigator as a word-spinner and a star-gazer, of no use to them at all?'

What Plato was getting at would be labelled by later generations as the 'tyranny of the majority'. Democracy leads to chaos, and order can only be restored by an option even worse than democracy – the pure tyranny of a single despotic ruler.

The guardians

Therefore, Plato said, the state should be led by its own star-gazer – a Philosopher-King, selected from an elite class of experts, known as 'guardians'. Potential guardians would be plucked from their families at a young age and sent to a commune. They would spend some time in the military, before dedicating themselves to the study of philosophy from the age of 30 – because only philosophers knew true human virtues, whereas everyone else was merely mimicking them. To prevent corruption, guardians would be banned from owning anything. (Philosophers would never be corrupt anyway because all that time thinking would have given them special access to the things that make people decent, Plato argued.) A modern way of putting this might be 'benign dictatorship' or the governments of technocrats that get installed when countries find themselves in a crisis. A modern response might be: 'We've had enough of experts.'

Plato identified what the academic Paul Corcoran describes as 'the perversity of democratic constitutions, the disorderliness of democratic politics and the moral depravity of the democratic character'. That was the view of democracy that stuck for centuries. Later, Aristotle's work was rediscovered in universities springing up across Europe in the Middle Ages and in the form of commentaries by the Muslim scholar Abū al-Walīd Muhammad ibn Ahmad ibn Muhammad ibn Rushd, also known as Averroës, who was active in Seville, Cordoba and Marrakesh. The Dominican priest Thomas Aquinas quoted Aristotelian concepts as he sought to fuse together religion and philosophy; Marsilius of Padua used them in his argument that the Pope should stick to religion and not governing; and Niccolò Machiavelli drew on them as he began formulating his argument that successful rulers had to be cunning to be kind in Florence in the early 16th century.

The condensed idea
Democracy as a boozy cruise

03 The Social Contract

A politician issues a list of pledges with her signature at the bottom. A French protestor says they have paid into the system all their life and so raising the retirement age is unfair. Whether conscious of the fact or not, the politician and protestor are both referencing the *social contract*, a way of thinking about the relationship between the people and their rulers that began in the 17th century. If you give up some of your rights, what do you get in return?

The sovereign

Political philosophy has only a few killer catchphrases, but English philosopher Thomas Hobbes came up with one of the greatest: 'Solitary, poor, nasty, brutish, and short.' He was referring to what he called humanity's 'state of nature' – life before there were any rules. Because resources are scarce, because human beings are just bodies in constant motion and because the only way a person can guarantee their security is by attacking first, life in the state of nature is 'war of all against all'.

This can be avoided if people agree among themselves to hand total power to a *sovereign* – which could be a person or a group of people or an assembly – in return for the guarantee of protection. 'A common power to keep them all in awe.' Often misunderstood, Hobbes's social contract is the deal struck *within* the population, rather than the one between the leader and the led.

Government

English philosopher John Locke, who was exiled to France and the Netherlands because he was opposed to the Catholic James II inheriting the Crown from his brother Charles II, had a much more optimistic view of human nature. He felt that Hobbesian absolute rule was a form of slavery. He argued that human beings could use reason and follow laws, and that they possessed innate natural rights – to 'life, liberty and estate.' ('Estate' meaning possessions in general, not just a country house with grounds.)

The problem was that, as populations grew and private property proliferated, there was a need for a neutral arbiter to settle disputes – a government. But in his *Two Treatises of Government* in 1689, Locke argued for a limited one that filled in the gaps in the state of nature, which preserved peace and property rights, and managed public goods. In what was effectively the birth of liberalism, Locke summarized the powers of the state as:

'the right of making Laws with Penalties of Death, and consequently all less Penalties, for the Regulating and Preserving of Property, and of employing the force of the Community, in the Execution of such Laws and in defence of the Common-wealth from Foreign Injury, and all this only for the Publick Good.'

A government would be legitimate if the population had agreed among themselves to have one, if it kept their consent and if power could be taken back.

Freedom and equality

Born in Geneva and then a leading member of the philosophical elite in Paris in the 1740s, Jean-Jacques Rousseau also had a favourable view of the state of nature. In it, man was – his words, not mine – 'a noble savage'. In fact, it was the development of society that had

---

Alternatives to social contract theory

The social contract theorists based much of their thinking on the idea that human beings are born with 'natural rights' such as Locke's guarantees of 'life, liberty, and estate'. 'Nonsense on stilts' replied the English philosopher Jeremy Bentham, who founded the doctrine of utilitarianism in the second half of the 18th century, in opposition to the school of natural rights after a dispute with a judge about whether laws were natural or man-made. Bentham's big thought was that society should be organized to maximize 'the greatest happiness of the greatest number'. Defining 'happiness' and 'the greatest number' has proved tricky ever since.

John Rawls developed his alternative model of society at Princeton University in the 1960s. He gave up the priesthood for academia after his experience fighting in the Second World War caused a crisis of faith. His theory of justice began by asking what sort of society we would build if we did not know in advance the position we would have in the pecking order. Surely if you knew you might be at the bottom, you would make sure that it was not too unpleasant? He also coined the 'difference principle', which argued that inequality is only justified if it leads to an improvement in the conditions of the worst off.

---

ruined things, especially the potentially massive inequalities that were created when some people owned property while others did not. Hence, his work *The Social Contract* began with the famous words 'Man is born free, and everywhere he is in chains'. Society's existing contract was unequal and therefore fraudulent and should be replaced with one in which all are equal. The *people* could be the sovereign, although people can be 'forced to be free', Rousseau asserted, controversially.

Beyond this the state could take on the political project of making people improved versions of themselves – a shocking idea at the time and one of the reasons Rousseau's work was banned in his native Geneva. Rousseau feared direct rule by the public because he did not think the population was intelligent enough. Instead, he favoured compulsory participation by the people in assemblies, where individual desires were subordinated to the 'general will' of society at large. It does not take a political genius to realize that these ideas could be used to justify some bad things. The French Revolution, anyone?

Sign . . . where?

There have been plenty of criticisms of social contract theory. Where are the moments in history that mark a signing of such a contract? If the social contract is tacitly accepted when you receive the benefits that flow from it, what if you do not want the benefits and did not ask for them? Were women, people of colour and the poor given the opportunity to opt out of a mostly white, male construct that disadvantaged them? Do you have to leave the country if you do not agree with the contract? The various thinkers behind versions of the social contract were big influences in the American and French Revolutions. Now, it feels that the social contract has become a metaphor for the services a person receives from their government in return for their taxes, rather than a high-minded debate about what the state is.

The condensed idea
A new deal?

04 American Independence

A violent break from Britain. The Declaration of Independence. The Constitution. The Bill of Rights. Combined, these events seem to represent a massive explosion of democratic freedoms. But the Founding Fathers of the United States were less concerned with building a democracy; more a republic that guarded against tyranny – the tyranny of a colonial master, an over-mighty federal government or by the people themselves.

No taxation without representation

From 1764, the British Parliament began passing laws that would apply taxes directly in its 13 American colonies. Sugar, newspapers and even playing cards became more expensive. This encouraged most of the colonies to meet for their first 'congress', which began the process of putting the 'United' in the United States. George Washington was appointed the commander-in-chief of the army that would eventually fight the war against the British from 1775–83. Initially it seemed the tension could be managed within a reformed British Empire, but in 1776 the colonists were roused to be more ambitious when British thinker Thomas Paine wrote in his pamphlet *Common Sense:* 'O ye that love mankind! Ye that dare oppose, not only the tyranny, but the tyrant, stand forth! Every spot of the old world is overrun with oppression. Freedom hath been hunted round the globe. Asia, and Africa, have long expelled her – Europe regards her like a stranger, and England hath given her warning to depart. O! receive the fugitive, and prepare in time an asylum for mankind.'

Declaring independence

The Continental Congress passed the Declaration of Independence from Britain in Philadelphia on the 4 July 1776. At the time, the focus of its main author, Thomas Jefferson, was more on listing grievances against George III. More significant now is the preamble that set out the moral basis of the future United States:

'We hold these truths to be self-evident, that all men are created equal, that they are endowed by their Creator with certain unalienable Rights, that among these are Life, Liberty and the pursuit of Happiness. That to secure these rights, Governments are instituted among Men, deriving their just powers from the consent of the governed. That whenever any Form of Government becomes destructive of these ends, it is the Right of the People to alter or to abolish it, and to institute new Government, laying its foundation on such principles and organizing its powers in such form, as to them shall seem most likely to effect their Safety and Happiness.'

Obviously the word 'equal' applies to men, not women or slaves. There is also a debate about whether 'happiness' was chosen over the word 'property' to paper over disagreements about slavery that would boil over in the Civil War of 1861–65. And the written constitution that would elaborate the 'Form of Government' would have to wait for another decade.

Framing the Constitution

For a few years the new nation muddled along with some articles of confederation that spelled out areas of cooperation, but there were growing calls for more substantial coordination. From May–September 1786, 55 delegates from the American elite met in Philadelphia, and decided to draft a new constitution for 'a government of laws and not of men'. They were broadly split between more radical followers of Thomas Jefferson, and more conservative supporters of George Washington and John Adams.

The theme that ran through the discussion was how to allocate the correct amount of power to central government, the states and the public . . . with a constant fear of giving the people too much of it. The delegates sought inspiration from ancient Rome and from the British monarchy they had just rejected. They settled on a six-page document of seven articles that created the three branches of government – a 'separation of powers' inspired by the French philosopher Baron de Montesquieu's idea of an insurance policy against despotism.

There would be a powerful Supreme Court. There would be an executive of a president and vice-president (elected by an Electoral College of state representatives, not directly by the people). The legislature would be a Congress of two houses, where each state got two seats in the Senate and a number relative to the size of their population in the lower House of Representatives. The latter would be the only part of the structure that was directly elected.

The advantages of this design were set out in a series of essays, known as *The Federalist* papers, written by the future President James Madison among others. In *Federalist* paper No. 10, Madison's main argument was that the new structure would prevent any particular 'faction' – property owners or an individual state, for instance – having too much power while allowing diversity and differences to flourish.

Is the Constitution democratic?

The academic Robert A Dahl noted seven 'important shortcomings' in the Constitution as a truly 'democratic' document:

1) It did not ban slavery or give Congress the power to do so; 2) States kept the power to decide who had the vote, effectively excluding women and African Americans. States could veto changes to the franchise; 3) It did not allow for the election of the president by the popular vote; 4) Senators would be selected by the state legislatures, not elected by the public; 5) Each state received two senators but seats in the House of Representatives were allocated based on population size. This combination meant that slave owners – a privileged minority – were over-represented; 6) The Supreme Court had the ability to strike down laws that had been approved democratically by Congress and the president; 7) Congress was not given the powers to approve things that ended up being quite important, such as the introduction of income tax or regulation of new industries such as banking.

Developments

To reassure sceptics of the Constitution, the framers quickly promised to introduce a Bill of Rights, a batch of ten amendments. The first guaranteed freedom of speech and assembly, the second the right of the people to bear arms (the origin of the fight over gun control), and the others mostly covered criminal justice. If the Constitution was the sword of more power for the federal government, the Bill of Rights was the shield to protect individuals from the state. The US

Many of the legendary figures from the early period of American democracy were spectacularly opposed to the idea of political parties because they would allow particular interests to dominate. In his farewell address as president, George Washington said they were 'likely . . . to become potent engines, by which cunning, ambitious, and unprincipled men will be enabled to subvert the power of the people'. But the Constitution itself gave rise to political parties – the Federalists who were in favour of it and the Democratic-Republicans who broadly supported the rights of states. Those two would rise, fall, split, disappear and be joined by the Whigs, The Know-Nothings and others before settling into the two-party system of modern times. The energy and excitement of early American life and politics leaps off the pages of *Democracy in America* by the French author Alexis de Tocqueville, who travelled across the country with a friend in 1831–32. His main observation was that America offered political equality to everyone, which was unique at the time but was likely to spread to Europe in de Tocqueville's assessment.

constitutional system was further shaped by battles over institutions such as a central banking system and whether to have a national debt.

Abraham Lincoln's description on the battlefield at Gettysburg in 1863 of 'government of the people, by the people, for the people' was more a promise than a reality, one that would develop through further amendments to the constitution over a century. The 12th amendment, in 1804, established direct elections for the president and vice-president. The 15th, in 1870, gave the vote to people of colour and former slaves, the 19th of 1920 gave the vote to women, and in 1971 the 26th amendment lowered the voting age to 18.

The condensed idea
Of the people, by the people, for the people . . . eventually

05 The French Revolution

I n Paris, on 27 June 1789, the English agriculturalist Arthur Young wrote: 'The whole business seems to be over . . . and the revolution is complete'. He clearly spoke too soon because the French Revolution would last for about a decade. But he had seen many of the pieces being put into place that would generate some of most momentous events in political history.

Freedom, equality, brotherhood

In the late 1780s the French state was bankrupt after a series of wars. It was also old-fashioned, ruled by an absolute monarch, Louis XVI, but fairly decentralized in terms of administration. Public office was bought and sold; taxes were avoided by rich and poor alike. Peasants were coerced into building and maintaining the roads under forced labour.

Various political and economic reforms to the creaking system coincided with a disastrous harvest, sending bread prices soaring. Louis XVI was pressured into summoning the Estates-General, an assembly where the nobility were represented in one 'estate', the clergy in the second and the general population in the third. But the third estate could be outvoted by the other two, leading to calls for greater representation of the people. The Estates-General morphed into a slightly more representative National Assembly. In May 1789 its members met on a tennis court in Versailles and agreed to write a constitution. A few weeks later they would announce the abolition of feudalism. The clock was ticking on the monarchy, on the entire system.

When Arthur Young made his rash prediction that 'the whole business seems to be over' in the summer of 1789, it would be weeks before the storming of the Bastille. The guillotine would be introduced three years later. Louis XVI would remain as king for a while longer, and the disorganized revolutionaries were not yet dreaming of a republic. There was yet to be a series of massacres – some would say a genocide – of opponents of the revolution in the Vendee in the west of France. There was violence and there were angry mobs but nothing like the bloodshed of The Terror of 1793–94, where tens of thousands of people were executed for opposing the revolution, often on the flimsiest pretext. The revolutionary leader Maximilien Robespierre was still working out the alternative calendar and the new religion he would introduce as part of wholesale change to French daily life. Napoleon was just a general in the army, not the emperor who would bring the great experiment to an end by ruling much like the monarch who had been overthrown.

Responses

The French set a vivid template for revolutions that has lived for centuries in the minds of historians, politicians, artists and the public. It proved that an old order – an *ancien regime* – could be overthrown in its entirety, with the power of the masses used as leverage against the existing elite. It reinforced ancient fears about democracy that giving too much power to the public could lead to chaos, and so some limits were required. For much of the 20th century the academic argument was whether the revolution had noble aims that got knocked off course and descended into violence, or whether the violence was built in from the start.

In his *Reflections on the Revolution in France*, the Irish-born writer and member of the British Parliament Edmund Burke predicted that there would be extreme bloodshed, leading to eventual dictatorship. He wrote the work in 1790, before most of the events unfolded, which earned him a reputation as a political soothsayer. *Reflections* is very quotable. Burke's reaction to the imprisonment of Queen Marie-Antoinette can be read as applying to the entire revolution:

'The Age of Chivalry is gone. That of sophisters, economists, and calculators has succeeded; and the glory of Europe is extinguished for ever. Never, never more, shall we behold the generous loyalty to rank and sex, that proud submission, that dignified obedience, that subordination of the heart, which kept alive, even in servitude itself, the spirit of an exalted freedom. The unbought grace of life, the cheap defence of nations, the nurse of manly sentiment and heroic enterprise is gone!'

Burke argued that social change had to be gradual and respectful of existing traditions, but also that some change was necessary because 'A state without the means of some change, is without the means of its own conservation.' To many, this was the birth of modern conservatism.

Burke's arguments were challenged by Thomas Paine after his return from America where he had encouraged the colonies to seek independence. He issued his pamphlet *The Rights of Man* in 1791. In it, Paine asserted that populations had to be able to overthrow their governments and replace them with new models that reflected the times:

> 'What were formerly called revolutions were little more than a change of persons . . . what we now see in the world, from the revolutions of America and France is a renovation of the natural order of things.'

The events in France and America were inevitable elsewhere, so better to anticipate them rather than 'commit them to the issue of convulsions', he wrote. Paine's pamphlets provided inspiration for the authors of the US Constitution and fuelled the fight to extend the right to vote in the United Kingdom. These arguments also earned him a charge of sedition – the incitement of rebellion.

Bill of Rights

The French Revolution also gave the world the idea of universal human rights. The National Assembly was renamed the National Constituent Assembly and, on 26 August 1789, it issued the Declaration of The Rights of Man and Citizens – the guarantees that would be provided by the upcoming constitution. After multiple re-writes, the document offered the right to freedom from oppression, security and the protection of property, equality in treatment by the state, freedom of expression and thought, and the rule of law. This was unprecedented because it went much further than equivalents elsewhere, such as the English Bill of Rights of 1689. Also, it applied to man as a species, not exclusively the French. Hence why it was copied heavily by the authors of the Universal Declaration of Human Rights in the 1940s. The European Convention on Human Rights of the 1950s uses very similar words and ideas, too.

Left and right

During hearings of the National Assembly, supporters of the revolution generally sat to the left of the chair and supporters of the monarchy sat to the right. This is often cited as the origin of the modern political spectrum, where 'left-wingers' care about inequality and 'right-wingers' favour the status quo. Clearly this is a vast simplification of a situation that included myriad factions with names such as Jacobins, Girondists, Hébertists, Dantonists and the *Enrages*, some of whom used the poor more as a tool than a cause. Like many of the products of the French Revolution it is a powerful idea that has been used, abused and misunderstood ever since – just like Marie-Antoinette's famous line about cake, which she probably never said; like the storming of the Bastille, which freed only seven prisoners, not an army of them; and like Victor Hugo's *Les Misérables*, which is set during the temporary restoration of the Bourbon monarchy in a different century.

The condensed idea
Liberté, égalité, fraternité

06 Universal Suffrage

During the Roman Republic, the Latin word *suffrigium* seems to have switched meanings between 'the right to participate' and 'the ability to buy positions of influence'. This is a good reminder that gaining the right to vote – suffrage – is a process, frequently a fight, and is sometimes less a noble act and more a political expedient. According to the website Our World in Data, around a third of the world's population lived in countries where they could vote in free and fair elections in 2021. The stories of three countries show how this right was extended to men, women and minorities.

Suffrage for men

Britain prides itself on having one of the world's oldest parliaments, but the extension of the right to vote was fairly recent, and initially only applied to men. It was also very gradual: 3 per cent of the adult population in 1883, then 16 per cent in 1867 ... 29 per cent in 1884 ... and 50 per cent in 1918. It proves the claim that the country does not do revolutions. The changes happened via a series of Great Reform Acts and through the enormous grassroots campaign of the Chartists.

The first Great Reform Act of 1832 extended the franchise to the male middle classes by loosening the requirement that voters had to own property of a certain value or pay a given amount of rent. In came new constituencies representing growing industrial cities, such as Manchester, and out went the 'pocket' boroughs where landowners could send their own personal representative to Parliament and the 'rotten' boroughs, such as Old Sarum, in Wiltshire, where there was a field, no houses and two members of parliament . . . who were brothers. (Progress on votes for women actually went backwards because this act explicitly excluded them for the first time. And the legislation only passed thanks to some politicking over which party could have more seats in the unelected House of Lords for backing it.)

This was not even close to enough for the working-class Chartist movement. The Chartists issued an ambitious list of six demands in 1838: all men to have the vote, voting by secret ballot, annual parliamentary elections, equal-sized constituencies, salaries for MPs, and the abolition of the rule that only property owners could become

MPs. Calling the Chartists a 'movement' fails to do justice to something that became more like a lifestyle for millions of people who read Chartist newspapers, attended Chartist rallies in vast numbers, worshipped in Chartist chapels and named their children after Chartist heroes, even calling some of them 'Charter'.

Further Great Reform Acts in 1867 and 1884, the Representation of the People Act in 1918, solving the problem of the disenfranchisement of men who had served abroad in the First World War, and the partial success of the suffragette and suffragist movements meant that, by 1918, five of the six Chartist demands had been met, and women over 30 could vote. All that was missing were annual elections.

Suffrage for women

In 1893, New Zealand became the first country in the world to give women the right to vote in national elections. It was the result of a combination of factors. The indigenous Maori shared roles more equally between men and women, providing a local model of greater equality. Upper-class men condescendingly thought that women would provide a civilizing counterbalance in a population that was skewed towards rowdy young men. There was an organization that could pursue women's rights alongside an already hot topic – the temperance movement, which combined their campaign for female votes with their demands to ban alcohol. And there was an energetic figurehead, Kate Sheppard, the country's first female newspaper owner and editor.

Around a quarter of the female population signed a petition, demonstrating wide public support, and the legislation was approved after a behind-the-scenes parliamentary fumble during which the premier's actions convinced two opponents to switch their votes at the

'Is it right that while the gambler, the drunkard, and even the wife-beater has a vote, earnest, educated and refined women are denied it? . . . Is it right . . . that a mother . . . should be thought unworthy of a vote that is freely given to the blasphemer, the liar, the seducer and the profligate?'

Kate Sheppard, in a pamphlet titled 'Is It Right?'

last minute. The additional right for women to be elected as members of parliament was abandoned as too much to ask, and that would not change for another 26 years.

Suffrage for African Americans

Even though African American men gained the right to vote with the passage of the 15th Amendment to the US Constitution in 1870, this was more theoretical than real because many southern states imposed restrictions, such as tests of language or 'moral character'. After three voting rights activists were murdered by the Ku Klux Klan in Mississippi in 1964 and white state troopers opened fire on Black marchers in Selma, Alabama, on Bloody Sunday in 1965, President Johnson signed the Voting Rights Act (VRA). Among the act's sections, three were of particular significance:

• Section 2 of the VRA backed up the constitutional right to vote with the full legal and political might of the federal government. This shifted the balance of power on voters' rights that had been given to the states in the Constitution.
• Section 5 forced states to receive the approval (or 'pre-clearance') of a court or the Attorney-General before they could introduce any law that might restrict voting on the basis of race. This granted the federal government a veto on voting policies.
• Section 4(b) laid out the conditions that defined which states were subject to the pre-clearance rule.

African American participation in elections almost trebled after the introduction of the VRA.

Voters' rights have become a legal and political pass-the-parcel between Congress and the Supreme Court in the decades since. A landmark judicial ruling came in 2013 during the presidency of Barack Obama. In Shelby v Holder, a majority of the court ruled that the discrimination of 1965 was a relic of the past, and so Section 4(b) of the Voting Rights Act had become an unwarranted intrusion into the rights of states by the federal government. The liberal judges on the court disagreed, with Ruth Bader Ginsburg writing in a dissenting opinion that this was 'like throwing away your umbrella in a rainstorm because you are not getting wet'. As a result, nine states with a history of discrimination were free to pass new laws on voting, which many activists deemed racist and some of which were sent to the Supreme Court. And the temperature of the conversation rose significantly when Donald Trump made evidence-free claims that he lost the 2020 election because of voter fraud.

The right to vote feels like a fundamental element of democracy, like oxygen or hydrogen in the periodic table. But in the past, and in some places now, such as the United States and India, it feels more like a product of factors, a chemical reaction that needs to be sustained.

The condensed idea
The fight for the right to vote

07 The Communist Manifesto

Karl Marx was a newspaper journalist and Friedrich Engels combined writing with managing his family's textiles business in Manchester. They did not invent the idea of communism. They did not create the communist movement. But they authored a powerful blueprint for it when they wrote the Communist Manifesto in 1848 as a response to arguments within the movement.

It was in 1848 that various authorities had brutally supressed popular uprisings all across Europe – in Paris, Berlin, Geneva, Stockholm and many other cities. The manifesto was written as a challenge to the way communism was being portrayed by those elites. In the opening to the document, Marx and Engels described it as an answer to the 'nursery tale' about a 'spectre' that was supposedly haunting the continent.

Triumph of the bourgeoisie

The first section of the manifesto was an explanation of how capitalism and business owners – 'the bourgeoisie' – had come to dominate the working class. Marx and Engels were impressed with what the capitalist system had achieved, writing: 'It has accomplished wonders far surpassing Egyptian pyramids, Roman aqueducts and Gothic cathedrals; it has conducted expeditions that put in the shade all former exoduses of nations and crusades'. They paint a picture of a restless economic system that is constantly inventing new things so that 'all that is solid melts into air' and that roams across the world seeking new markets.

But the system as it stood was prone to crises. It was so productive that it often *over*-produced. This drove down prices and caused cut-throat competition. Parts of the system were destroyed and then had to be rebuilt. And the capitalists did not understand what they had created, because they were like 'the sorcerer who is no longer able to control the powers of the nether world whom he has called up by his spells'.

The modern state was simply a 'committee' to maintain this state of affairs. And it was all built on the exploitation of labour, the proletariat. The way the bourgeoisie made their profits was by driving down the value and quality of work so that the workers become 'an appendage to the machine'. This meant they were no longer fit to be in charge because the conditions of the proletariat were getting worse and worse. But because the workers had been forced to live in towns, they were beginning to organize themselves so that they could challenge the system: 'What the bourgeoisie therefore produces, above all, are its own gravediggers. Its fall and the victory of the proletariat are equally inevitable.'

Marx and Engels' plan

The communists were the people who had seen most clearly what change was required, and believed in it most strongly, Marx and Engels argued in the Communist Manifesto. Their mission was summed up in one phrase: 'The abolition of private property'. The pair then used the manifesto to defend themselves from the accusations of their critics that they were seeking the end of possessions, the family, the role of women and of individual countries. Their argument for each was the same: the bourgeoisie and the capitalist system had destroyed all of these things already. Marx and Engels finally explained what had to be done, writing:

'The proletariat will use its political supremacy to wrest, by degrees, all capital from the bourgeoisie, to centralize all instruments of production in the hands of the State, i.e. of all the proletariat organized as a ruling class; and to increase the total of productive forces as rapidly as possible.

'Of course, in the beginning, this cannot be effected except by means of despotic inroads on the rights of property, and on the conditions of bourgeois production.'

Marx and Engels ended their manifesto with a list of ten policies to achieve this. These ranged from the abolition of land ownership and the right to inherit property, to the centralization of transport and communications in the hands of the state, to the creation of 'industrial armies' and the redistribution of the population more equally between town and country. The manifesto closes with the infamous rallying cry: 'WORKING MEN OF ALL COUNTRIES, UNITE!'

Marx did not specify in detail how a communist society would be run, but he was thrilled by the two-month democratic experiment of the Paris Commune in 1871 when the citizens took control of the city (population: 2 million). Marx listed the things he liked about the commune: everyone had a vote, officials of every level were paid the same living wage and could be easily replaced by the public, loan repayments were frozen and there was a ban on charging interest, the police were replaced by armed citizens. Marx wrote that the commune demonstrated that the working class could not just rely on grabbing 'the ready-made state machinery, and [wielding] it for its own purposes,' but revolution required that they 'smash' it. There could be no compromise.

What happened next?

It took a while for the Communist Manifesto to become influential. Then, as the scholar of Marx Gareth Stedman Jones wrote in his introduction to the edition published in 2002: '. . . the formulations of the manifesto underpinned the creation of a worldwide labour movement in the last third of the 19th century, and in the 20th century, fuelled many of the political struggles – and not a few of the wars – that tore the world apart from 1917–89.'

Historians have estimated that at its global peak in the middle of the 20th century, around a third of the world's population lived under regimes that could be described as communist. Just as Marx and Engels did not invent communism, Lenin, Stalin, Mao, Castro and others imposed their own interpretations of the Communist Manifesto on their people.

Marxism today?

Today, does the word 'Marxism' have more power to insult than to inspire? Take the Black Lives Matter (BLM) movement that was formed in 2015 and came to global prominence after police killed George Floyd in Minnesota in 2020. Critics of BLM often labelled them as Marxists, confident that the word would discredit them among mainstream opinion. One right-wing critique was titled 'The Making of a New Marxist Revolution'. In response, one of the co-founders of BLM's central organizing group, Patrisse Cullors, released a YouTube video titled 'Am I Marxist?' She explained she was campaigning for 'a socio-economic system that doesn't oppress some groups of people and only uplifts a few'. Her not-quite-yes-not-quite-no answer to the question was: 'I do believe in Marxism.'

The condensed idea
Workers of the world unite

08 Democratic Transitions

During half a century at Harvard University, the political scientist Samuel P Huntington founded the diplomats' favourite journal, *Foreign Affairs*, in 1970 and authored one of its most quoted articles in 1991. Written as the Soviet Union teetered on the brink of collapse, Huntingdon looked back at the spread of democracy and spotted that it came in three waves.

Huntington's three waves

According to Huntington, the first wave began in 1820 with the growth of male suffrage in the United States and ended in 1926 with 29 democracies established across the globe. But then came a reverse wave with the triumph of Mussolini in Italy and Hitler in Germany. The end of the Second World War saw the wave roar back and there were 36 democracies by 1962, including those imposed by the Allies in Germany and Japan. The years 1960–75 saw a second reversal, which reduced the number of democracies to 30. The pattern repeated with the arrival of third great wave of democratization which was triggered by the collapse of Portugal's military dictatorship in 1974.

Huntington attempted to explain what drove the tide of democracy. Authoritarian regimes had failed to deliver for their populations. A global economic boom meant people were richer, and wealthier people wanted more say. The Catholic Church, he argued, had switched from upholding the status quo to challenging authoritarianism. The democratic boom had also been encouraged by the foreign policies of the United States and European Community. And then there was 'snowballing' – the birth of a democracy here encouraged another one there. Ultimately, Huntington concluded, it came down to the courage and self-interest of those with power: 'History . . . does not sail ahead in a straight line, but when skilled and determined leaders are at the helm, it does move forward.'

Theories of democratization

Huntington was criticized as being too Western-centric, too naive and of having too simplistic a definition of democracy. A grand theory of the wave pattern that satisfies everyone is yet to be uncovered, despite a lot of research by academics. They agree that the timeline of democratization breaks down into a transition phase from something that does not look like democracy to something that does, followed by a consolidation phase where democratic processes and institutions take root, or fail to. Beyond this, the number of theories is almost endless, but they have clustered around some key concepts:

Economic Economic development seems to encourage democracy. This could be because a growing middle class expects greater representation in how their country is governed. Capitalism demands respect for property rights and the presence of the rule of law to guarantee contracts and transactions. History also suggests that authoritarian regimes falter when they cannot provide for their people.

Cultural When it comes to cultural factors, the debate can appear to be based on big generalizations about religion and race. A classic example is found in the writings of the American diplomat George Kennan, who wrote in the 1970s that democracy only existed in places that had been settled by people from northern Europe and so it had 'a relatively narrow base both in time and in space; and the evidence has yet to be produced that it is the natural form of rule for peoples outside those narrow perimeters.'

Chicken and egg These theories focus on the interplay between the factors that led to the democratic transition and the outcome of the transition itself. Did the remains of the outgoing regime negotiate with their opponents, a type of transition described as 'pacted'? Was there a revolution from the grassroots up? Did the country inherit some political institutions from a colonial power, or were institutions introduced from outside after a war? Another analytical tool is 'path dependency' – how pre-existing factors limit future options.

The Arab Spring

Many of these factors combined in the Tunisian city of Sidi Bouzid on 17 December 2010, when a fruit and vegetable seller named Mohamed Bouazizi set himself on fire in a protest about his treatment by officials in the market. It sparked the Jasmine Revolution, which led to the overthrow of the country's autocratic regime. This was followed by a

Trends in democratization are captured each year in indexes, including by the Economist Intelligence Unit (EIU), an arm of publishers of the *Economist* newspaper and the Variations of Democracy (V-Dem) project based in Gothenburg, Sweden. They assign countries to different categories – 'liberal democracies', 'electoral democracies' in the case of V-Dem, 'full democracies' and 'flawed democracies' at the EIU.

Both organizations agreed that, in 2022, the world was evenly split between the number of democracies and autocracies, although they came up with different numbers. And a majority of people lived in non-democracies when population size was taken into account, rather than just a raw number of governments. V-Dem calculated that the world was becoming more autocratic, reverting to levels seen in the 1990s. According to the EIU, global levels of democratization had stagnated. The EIU singled out Thailand as an example of a democratizing country. Researchers credited the increasing role of opposition political parties and the end of local insurgencies. The star performer in V-Dem's assessment was the Seychelles.

Digging into the data reveals some quirks in this methodology. In the V-Dem listings the number of 'electoral democracies' had increased, but only because some of the previously top-rated 'liberal democracies' had become *less* democratic and so were downgraded. Some countries improved their ratings under the EIU criteria, but only because they had restored freedoms that had temporarily been restricted due to COVID, not because democracy had flourished. V-Dem listed Greece as a country going backwards democratically; the EIU said Greece had made progress.

Rather than another wave of democratization, many observers have argued that the end of the Arab Spring, and crackdowns elsewhere, were actually part of fourth reverse wave of democratization. This erosion of democratic norms has been given the label 'backsliding'.

series of revolutions in countries across the Middle East and North Africa – in Egypt, Yemen, Syria, Libya and others. It was called the Arab Spring, an echo of the popular uprisings of 1848, known as the People's Spring and the protests against Communism in Eastern Europe in 1968, the Prague Spring. Some criticized this title as the invention of Western journalists and politicians, who had generalized a series of disparate events involving different communities, causes and factors as a Huntington-style fourth wave of democratization.

The revolts in Syria, Yemen and Libya became civil wars. Russia backed the Assad regime in Syria, Iran and Saudi Arabia influenced the conflict in Yemen, and the United States, United Kingdom and France intervened in Libya. The Egyptian dictator Hosni Mubarak was replaced and elections were held. The Muslim Brotherhood won but the country was paralyzed politically, leading to the military coup that brought President el-Sisi to power in 2013. The four-decade rule of the Libyan dictator Muammar Gaddafi ended with his death in 2011. A brief government of national unity was formed in 2020 but has struggled to implement the electoral system designed under the supervision of the United Nations.

Tunisia became one of the few Arab Spring countries to take steps towards genuine democracy when it held multiparty elections and introduced a new constitution in 2014. But in 2021 President Kais Saied granted himself extra powers using emergency measures, which became permanent after he issued a new constitution. Across the countries of the Arab Spring, living standards and press freedom have flatlined at best, and perceptions of corruption have increased. Stanford University's Larry Diamond used three words to describe what had happened to the dreams of the protestors: 'Thwarted, squandered, pre-empted'.

The condensed idea
The tide of democracy goes in and out

09 Brexit

The United Kingdom had held referendums before. It had even held referendums on staying in the club of integrated European nations before. But the vote on membership of the European Union held on 23 June 2016 challenged many of the norms of British politics and drew in all the institutions of this established, liberal, parliamentary democracy. A new name for the process had to be invented: Brexit, a combination of 'Britain' and 'exit'.

The choice

The question asked of the British public was: Should the United Kingdom remain a member of the European Union or leave the European Union? Some 33 million votes were cast. The option of leaving won by 52 per cent to 48 per cent. It meant 17,410,742 people voted for Brexit, more than for any political party in any general election, ever. But the binary nature of the decision meant there was no space for compromise: it was in or out of the EU. The only room for manoeuvre was on the type of future relationship to be negotiated with the European Union on trade, security, migration and other areas of shared interest.

In light of the closeness of the vote, the then prime minister, David Cameron, was criticized for not including a threshold for triggering such a momentous decision, say 60 per cent of eligible voters. Some also suggested that a second referendum on the terms of the United Kingdom's departure should have been promised at the time of the initial vote so that the public could change their minds if they did not like the end product.

Leadership in a parliamentary system

David Cameron announced his resignation as prime minister and leader of the Conservative Party the morning he lost the referendum. He was accused of leaving the country in the lurch, but it would have been difficult for him to deliver an outcome he had campaigned against so vigorously. Theresa May was chosen by Conservative MPs to succeed Cameron. She held a snap general election. But because of her lacklustre performance on the campaign trail, she failed to win a majority of the seats in the House of Commons. There would be huge consequences. She resigned after her Brexit deal was rejected by Parliament three times. May's replacement was Boris Johnson, who won a contest that was decided by the votes of MPs and Conservative party activists. He resigned in 2021 and was replaced by Liz Truss. She announced her resignation after 44 days in office and was replaced by Rishi Sunak. It meant the United Kingdom had five Prime Ministers in six years, only three of whom had won a general election.

A divided parliament

Because of Theresa May's weak election victory in 2017, the UK parliament was seriously divided during most of the Brexit era. This posed problems for the British system, where the government can only govern if it has the votes of enough members of parliament. This was compounded by divisions within the Conservative party over whether to pursue a close or distant future relationship with the EU. And there were divisions . . . everywhere. This became clear on the night of 27 March 2019, when none of eight possible Brexit options won enough votes. Boris Johnson's deal with the EU was only approved by MPs after he had held an election and won a majority in the House of Commons. At various points parliamentarians seized control of the parliamentary timetable so they could issue instructions to the government, reversing the traditional relationship between executive and legislature.

The courts

The United Kingdom's highest court intervened at several points. In the early days of the Brexit process it ruled that the referendum result was only 'advisory' on the government and therefore did not automatically give ministers the power to begin the process of leaving the EU, only a vote in parliament could. This triggered headlines from a Brexit-supporting newspaper which labelled the judges 'Enemies of the People'.

Later, when Boris Johnson suspended parliament for five weeks – a process known as 'prorogation' – judges ruled that he had exceeded his executive powers. Also, the decision to prorogue parliament was technically made by the Queen on the advice of the prime minister. This drew the monarch into the type of political

The EU had a lot of experience of international negotiations, giving it an advantage over the United Kingdom. It started preparations early and put in a lot of effort to prevent divisions between its 27 member countries, which could have weakend its position. EU countries resisted British attempts to divide and rule. The priority for Brussels was securing the orderly departure of the United Kingdom and so the first phase of negotiations focused on securing three things: the rights of EU nationals who had made their home in the United Kingdom, the long-term financial commitment made by the British government when it was a member, and the Irish border. In a move known as 'sequencing', the negotiations on the future trade relationship would only begin after those initial issues had been settled. The end products of the talks were a 177-page Withdrawal Agreement, which settled the terms of the divorce, and a 2,530-page Trade and Cooperation Agreement for everything else.

situation that is usually avoided by the British head of state under Britain's unwritten constitution.

The UK constitution

Brexit tested the relationship between the constituent nations of the UK. Majorities of the population in Scotland and Northern Ireland voted to remain in the EU; the opposite happened in England and Wales. Some questioned whether the referendum should have included a threshold of nations for it to pass.

Because Northern Ireland shares a border with Ireland – which is a member of the EU – this became the United Kingdom's only land frontier with the European Union. Legally this implied the construction of customs posts and other infrastructure. But the peace process on the island of Ireland is based on the idea that the border is invisible to people who live and trade across it. This became the central issue in the negotiations with the EU. It culminated in separate arrangements for Northern Ireland, including the continued application of some European law. This angered some Northern Irish people, who felt their links with the rest of the United Kingdom had been undermined.

The aftermath

The United Kingdom left the EU on 31 January 2020, entering an 11-month transition period during which nothing changed. Soon afterwards the world was hit by Covid and then the Russian invasion of Ukraine. This combination of events has made it difficult to judge the outcome of Brexit, beyond the political chaos it unleashed in the United Kingdom. Data is starting to suggest a mixed picture. Migration from the EU to the United Kingdom, of students and workers, has slumped, yet immigration from the rest of the world has risen. The United Kingdom lags its competitors in the export of goods now that trade with its neighbours has become more difficult, yet Britain's trade in services is booming. Disagreements between the United Kingdom and the EU over the special arrangements for Northern Ireland appear to have been resolved, but tensions remain within Northern Irish communities, and support for Northern Ireland's merger with Ireland appears to be increasing. One thing is certain: no other EU countries are currently contemplating their own version of Brexit.

The condensed idea
A simple question that tested an entire system

10 Liberal Democracy

Recognizing a liberal democracy can be likened to US Supreme Court Justice Potter Stewart's definition of obscenity in a 1964 pornography trial: 'I know it when I see it.' A decent attempt at a definition has been made by the political data analysts at the Regimes of the World project, who make an annual assessment of whether the world is getting more or less democratic.

A country earns the gold-star category of 'liberal democracy' from Regimes of the World if it has the six attributes compiled by noted theorist Robert Dahl – 1) a government that is elected; 2) free and fair elections without coercion; 3) freedom of expression with no fear of punishment for criticizing the government; 4) places to get reliable information such as newspapers; 5) the right to set up associations such as trade unions, political parties or campaign groups; and 6) no one is deprived of the right to participate in the first five. In addition, a liberal democratic country also has to have checks and balances on the executive through the courts and a legislature, plus protection of individual liberties and equality before the law.

Even though they are not solely the product of liberal parties or people who identify as liberals, the history of *liberalism* explains that liberal democracies are defined by equality, the right of the individual and limits to the authority of the state, with democratic ideas of voting and political representation attached.

The liberal tradition

In the 17th century, John Locke effectively invented the idea of a limited government that had the consent of the public, concerning itself only with matters for the public good and not the private lives of its citizens. The idea of awarding rights to those who were not wealthy white men started to spread when Mary Wollstonecraft published her *Vindication of the Rights of Woman* in 1792. In the 19th century John Stuart Mill turbocharged the entire liberal tradition with *On Liberty*, which popularized the idea that states were only justified in limiting a person's freedom if that person's behaviour posed a risk to others – the 'harm principle' – and gave a stirring defence of the right to freedom of speech and thought. All this, Mill wrote, meant the individual was free to experiment with life to the benefit of humanity:

> 'As it is useful that while mankind is imperfect there should be different opinions, so it is that there should be different experiments in living; that free scope should be given to varieties of character, short injury to others; and that the worth of different modes of life should be proved practically . . . [That is] quite the ingredient of individual and social progress.'

The trade-offs inherent within a liberal democracy were summed up neatly in 1969, in an essay by the philosopher Isaiah Berlin. His famous formula balanced negative liberty (the right to be free from interference) and positive liberty (the right to pursue your goals and your autonomy) with the warning that the latter could be used politically to reduce the former. If that discussion seems overly theoretical, think of the agonies in liberal democracies over lockdowns in the early 2020s. Lockdowns were reductions of negative liberty to protect the positive liberty of not dying from Covid or from an overloaded health service.

The triumph of liberal democracy?

Liberal democracy outlived all alternatives to become the most successful way of organizing societies, argued the historian Francis Fukuyama in his 1989 paper *The End of History*. He cited Mikhail Gorbachev's introduction of economic and political reforms in the Soviet Union as proof that communism was doomed. The paper was followed by a book in 1992 after the USSR had finally been dissolved. Fukuyama has spent the decades since correcting misunderstandings about what he meant. His description of history 'ending' does not mean that events will stop happening, but harks back to Hegel, the German philosopher. Hegel believed that history progressed in a way that felt like . . . progress, which Marx built on to predict that communism would be humanity's stable end state.

The collapse of communism, the defeat of fascism in the Second World War and the failure of regimes based on nationalism or religion to go viral among the rest of humanity showed that liberal democracy was the only model that held genuine appeal, Fukuyama argued. He is wistful about this rather than triumphant, predicting:

'... the worldwide ideological struggle that called forth daring, courage, imagination and idealism will be replaced by economic calculation, the endless solving of technical problems, environmental concerns and the satisfaction of sophisticated consumer demands.'

He summarized the winning ideology as 'liberal democracy in the political sphere combined with easy access to VCRs and stereos in the economic'. The age of TikTok and AirPods has forced Fukuyama to

Neoliberalism

Are liberal democracies really *neo*-liberal democracies? In the purest sense, the political and economic doctrine of neoliberalism was a return to the ideas of the original liberals who emphasized industry and trade, and who promoted the protection of private property rather than equality and human rights. An early proponent was the economist Friedrich Hayek. Reacting to the 'big government' ideologies of communism, fascism and social democracy in the mid-20th century, Hayek argued that the free market was the only guarantee of freedom because anything else inevitably led to an overbearing state that took more and more powers to satisfy the endless demands of different groups.

This set the scene for the deregulation, privatization and innovation of the 1970s onwards. Neoliberalism holds different meanings for different people, depending where they are on the scale between libertarian crypto trader and social-justice direct activist. So, too, with the word 'liberal': in Germany it means on the right; in Canada it is the left; in the United States it might be a badge of honour that defines what news channel a person watches, or form the basis of the insult 'libtard' used online by right-wing trolls to describe someone with broadly 'liberal' views.

carry out a system update. He now says that the dominance of liberal democracy is being challenged by the rise of authoritarian capitalism in China.

And what do those political data geeks say about the supposed march of liberal democracy? The Regimes of the World team calculated that the number of liberal democracies peaked in 2009 at 42 and fell to 32 in 2022. A billion people could say they were living in liberal democracies but twice as many – 2.2 billion – found themselves in 'closed autocracies'. The causes and consequences of this are the political story of this century.

Others would argue that there is not necessarily a link between liberalism and democracy. Political scientist Philippe Schmitter wrote: 'Liberalism, either as a conception of political liberty, or as a doctrine about economic policy, may have coincided with the rise of democracy. But it has never been immutably or unambiguously linked to its practice'. For CNN anchor and former editor of *Newsweek*, Fareed Zakaria, the conflation of the two into one package meant that liberal democracy became less of a descriptive category and more like 'a badge of honour' to be smugly withheld or patronizingly bestowed on other countries. He made the case that: 'The absence of free and fair elections should be viewed as one flaw, not the definition of tyranny.'

The condensed idea
Today's democracies are based on liberal principles

11 Representative Democracy

Decision-making by everyone, ancient Athenian-style, can lead to mob rule and is impractical in the modern era, where populations are large and public policy problems are hard. But decision-making by one person is dictatorial and undemocratic. If this is the problem, then the answer is representative democracy, where elected representatives make decisions on behalf of their constituents and are held accountable at regular elections.

Elements of representation were scattered like crumbs throughout the history of democracy before it became the default. Ancient Rome had its tribunes, with leaders who were a little like elected prime ministers. Medieval monarchs in the Netherlands, England and Sweden would summon nobles to add legitimacy to their demands for new taxes, usually when they were about to start a war. In the 16th century the Swedish King Gustav Vasa included the peasantry in his consultations, alongside the nobility, the clergy and notables from towns, establishing the idea that someone could be worthy of representation even if they were not a rich landowner.

In broad terms the French and American revolutions started because populations felt decisions were being made about them, without them, embodied by the slogan of the American colonists, 'No taxation without representation'. To make it very obvious to everyone, the US Constitution created a House of *Representatives*, which the second US president John Adams said 'should be in miniature, an exact portrait of the people at large. It should think, feel, reason and act like them'. His fellow framer of the US constitution, James Madison, thought that representation was 'the cure' to the domination of a majority over a minority. And the hugely influential thinker on modern democracy, John Stuart Mill, gave one of his most important works the title *Considerations on Representative Government* (1861).

Representative or delegate?

A huge dilemma has dominated discussions about representative democracy. Are the people doing the job in the parliament, assembly, or whichever representative body a democracy has created for itself, meant to be *delegates*, who faithfully translate the wishes of their constituents? Or are they supposed to act independently and use their judgment to reach the best decisions for society as a whole? The most famous case for the latter was made by the Irishman Edmund Burke when he was elected as the Member of Parliament for the English city of Bristol. In his close-of-polling speech, he told his constituents: 'Your representative owes you, not his industry only, but his judgment; and he betrays, instead of serving you, if he sacrifices it to your opinion'. He went on:

> 'Parliament is not a congress of ambassadors from different and hostile interests; which interests each must maintain, as an agent and advocate, against other agents and advocates; but parliament is a deliberative assembly of one nation, with one interest, that of the whole; where, not local purposes, not local prejudices, ought to guide, but the general good, resulting from the general reason of the whole. You choose a member, indeed; but when you have chosen him, he is not member of Bristol, but he is a member of parliament.'

As persuasive as Burke has been for many professional politicians since, the debate has continued about the extent to which representatives are supposed to channel the desires of their constituents. Although he was referring to governments taking unpopular decisions, the former prime minister of Luxembourg Jean-Claude Juncker also managed to encapsulate the representative's dilemma when he said: 'We all know what to do, but we don't know how to get re-elected once we have done it.'

Rethinking representation

Political scientists' attempts to grapple with this have led to a vast literature. Hanna Pitkin came up with a useful framework at the University of California, Berkeley in the 1960s as the campus was gripped by student activism and protests against the Vietnam War. She invented four categories. Formalistic representation is the structure that allows representation to happen, such as how people are elected and then how they are held to account. More philosophically, symbolic representation is the meaning that the elected hold for the electors. Descriptive representation is the extent to which the politicos resemble the people that put them in parliament in terms of class, gender, race and so on. Substantive representation covers the things that representatives do – or fail to do – once they take office. Harvard Professor Jane Mansbridge added a few more. Anticipatory representation is when politicians behave in ways designed to win

Fairer representation

Another issue is whether a single representative, or a group of them, can ever truly represent the diversity of the society that they serve. Countries have found different ways to try to make their legislatures more accurately mirror their populations. In New Zealand members of the Maori minority can add themselves to a specific list of voters, who elect Maori members of parliament. The British Labour Party selects its candidates for some elections from all-female shortlists, and Rwanda has a legally mandated minimum number of female members of parliament.

In the United States the Voting Rights Act of 1965 has been used to create 'majority-minority' districts for elections to the House of Representatives. This means that electoral boundaries can be redrawn to turn racial or language minorities into a majority of the electorate, rather than being 'submerged' within another, larger community. A landmark court case in 1983 set out three tests for when this is justified: the minority community must be politically cohesive, sufficiently large but geographically compact and there has to be evidence that the majority has acted en bloc, preventing the minority from electing the candidates it wanted.

No parliament has yet pursued the eye-catching idea proposed by free-marketeer Friedrich Hayek. He suggested that someone should only be eligible for election if they were no longer too young to be inexperienced but not too old that they had stopped caring about the future. He suggested the ideal age was 45. This happened to be the age he was when he wrote his most influential work, *The Road to Serfdom*.

them approval at the next election instead of delivering on their promises from the last one. Surrogate representation is when they act on behalf of interests outside the geographical area that they represent. And 'gyroscopic' representation is when they represent their own values because they 'act like gyroscopes, rotating on their own axes, maintaining a certain direction, pursuing certain built-in (although not fully immutable) goals'.

Opponents of representation

Some famous political thinkers have opposed the whole idea of representative democracy. Jean-Jacques Rousseau thought it was impossible for a group of people to represent the will of all of the people. He argued:

> 'The people of England regards itself as free; but it is grossly mistaken; it is free only during the election of members of parliament. As a soon as they are elected, slavery overtakes it, and it is nothing.'

The father of anarchism Pierre-Joseph Proudhon looked back in horror at his typical day as an elected representative in the French National Assembly in 1848. He started at 9am, finished late in the evening and attended meetings constantly, which left him out of touch with reality. 'One must have lived in the isolator that is called a National Assembly to realize how the men who are most completely ignorant of the state of the country are almost always those who represent it', he wrote.

The condensed idea
One represents many

12 Majoritarian Democracy

Representing the wishes of a majority of the people the majority of the time; as features of democracy are supposed to go this one is pretty . . . major. In the 18th century, the father of modern government John Locke wrote that a community could only come together and act as 'one Body' by 'the will and determination of the majority'. And the Body could only move 'whither the greater force carries it, which is the consent of the majority; or else it is impossible it should act or continue one Body . . .'

Mathematical majorities

This philosophical concept appeared to receive scientific backing in 1785, when the French mathematician Marie-Jean-Antoine-Nicolas de Caritat, marquis of Condorcet, came up with his jury theorem. He proved that the more people involved in making a decision, the more likely it was to be correct. If the average person knew enough to choose the right answer to a question, then a *group* of people would be even more likely to come to the right conclusion. He showed, for example, that if an individual has a 55 per cent chance of being right then the chance of 399 people being right rose to . . . 98 per cent.

Here was proof of the wisdom of crowds, just as the crowd was about to go wild in the French Revolution. But the theory only worked on two conditions. Firstly, that the average person is likely to choose wisely. Secondly, that they act impartially rather than in their own self-interest or after being lobbied by someone else.

Major problems

Those heroic assumptions about human nature are at the heart of the oldest criticisms of democratic decision-making by majority vote. Either, that it places too much power in the hands of people who are not qualified (the elitist argument made by Plato). Or that it tramples over minorities (made from the left by thinkers such as John Rawls) or individuals (made from the right by Hayek, who argued that there could theoretically be more freedom under some dictatorships than in a 'doctrinaire democracy'). Even idealistic Rousseau – whose entire theory rested on the delivery of the General Will, remember –

stipulated that for a system to work, populations should be choosing what was good for society as whole, not satisfying their own whims.

Tyranny of the majority

This issue was labelled succinctly by Alexis de Tocqueville, who coined the 'tyranny of the majority' during a nine-month gap year in the United States, which he began in 1831. The Frenchman identified

The Westminster Model

'Majoritarian' is also the name given to a model of government, where one party rules because it has a majority over the other parties in the legislature. The British model is the prime example of this. The United Kingdom's first-past-the-post (FPTP) electoral system can give a political party a very big share of MPs in the House of Commons on the basis of a much smaller percentage of the votes in the country. The accusation is that this grants the prime minister almost unlimited powers to pass new laws that face hardly any challenge in the House of Commons (which they control), or the House of Lords (which is weak). The prime minister can also call an election whenever they want.

To advocates of strong government, this is what the people want – strong government. To critics it is more like 'an elective dictatorship', as Lord Hailsham memorably described it in a lecture in 1976. Recent leaders such as David Cameron, Theresa May and Boris Johnson probably did not feel very dictatorial while they were being pushed around by Parliament, the courts and their own colleagues. Less Stalin, more like Mr Bean, to borrow an old Westminster joke.

And while the British government set-up can be described as majoritarian, the electoral system cannot. A Member of Parliament does not need to win 50 per cent plus one of the votes – an absolute majority. Rather they are elected if they win more votes than their opponents – an outcome that is technically known as a 'plurality'.

several consequences: government was unstable because it constantly passed new laws to satisfy the 'passing passions' of voters, there was a conformity to public opinion, which stifled free speech, Native and African Americans were oppressed, and there were outbreaks of violence, such as lynching or the murder of newspaper journalists opposed to the war against the British in 1812, for example. He asked:

> 'When a man or party suffers from an injustice in the United States, to whom can he turn? To public opinion? That is what forms the majority. To the legislative body? That represents the majority and obeys it blindly. To the executive power? That is appointed by the majority and serves as its passive instrument. To the public police force? They are nothing but the majority under arms. To the jury? That is the majority invested with the right to pronounce judgment; the very judges in certain states are elected by the majority.'

Taming the majority

To a certain extent, the whole recent history of democracy has been about finding answers to de Tocqueville's questions. The solutions he identified in the United States included the power of voluntary associations, religion, the strong local identities he found in American towns and villages, and the fact that a large number of people and institutions were involved in making the system work. These amounted to 'so many hidden reefs that hold back or separate the flood of the people's will'. More broadly speaking, the solutions that have been pursued since have boiled down to developing tools that balance 'majority rule and minority rights'.

Also, what if the majority is not even a majority in the first place? John Stuart Mill imagined a situation where 'there is a contested election in every constituency, and every election is carried by a small majority. The Parliament this brought together represents little more than a bare majority of the people. This Parliament proceeds to legislate, and adopts important measures by a bare majority of itself.' He recommended a system of proportional voting, which seems fairly reasonable to many people. And as an insurance policy, that the educated got to vote multiple times, which seems reasonable to very few. Hannah Arendt wrote that the rise of the Nazis via the parliamentary process exploded some myths about European democracy. Namely, by showing that the 'majority' that participated in elections were really a minority because the 'politically neutral and indifferent masses' sat them out. This meant that democratic governments had rested as much on the silent approval of the 'inarticulate' citizens as on the active ones who made a noise about democracy. Therefore opponents of democracy could convince 'the people at large that parliamentary majorities were spurious and did not necessarily correspond to the realities of the country'.

And if the problem of a majority ruling over a minority is ever present then maybe, as British philosopher Richard Wollheim wrote, 'we should mean something different by "ruling"?'

The condensed idea
What if the majority is wrong?

13 Direct Democracy

Are political decisions more legitimate if you cut out the middleman of the elected representative and allow the public to do the deciding? The ancient Athenians thought so then and advocates of various forms of direct democracy do now, especially as technology has opened up the potential to reach nearly all of the people, nearly all of the time.

Marx

One of the most vigorous proponents of direct democracy was Karl Marx. This is often overlooked because he used the much misunderstood phrase 'the dictatorship of the proletariat' to describe one of the stages on the journey from capitalism to communism and because Marxist leaders such as Lenin, Stalin and Mao ran repressive regimes. Marx believed that neither the state nor politics itself could be neutral because both upheld the unequal power relations between capitalists and workers, and so therefore both the state and politics had to be replaced. He did not give detailed instructions for an alternative because he believed 'the music of the future' could not be composed in advance. But, inspired by the short-lived Paris Commune of 1871, Marx favoured a pyramid structure of elected delegates who were directly answerable to the people. A basic administrator would oversee it, and no one would contest elections because everyone agreed on everything. To Marxist critic Tony Polan, writing at the height of the Cold War in the 1980s, Marx had been hopelessly naive:

'It is . . . a gigantic gamble; the gamble that it will be possible to set about constructing the state in the "best of all possible worlds". The odds against the gamble are astronomic . . . It also demands a situation devoid of all political conflict, of all economic problems, of all sorts of contradictions, of all inadequate, selfish or simply human emotions and motivations, of all singularity, of all negativity. It demands, in short . . . an absence of politics.'

Referendums

The best-established tool of direct democracy in modern states is the referendum, a public vote on a single political question. (They are also known as plebiscites, from the Latin word *plebs*, meaning 'common people'. In Australia a referendum alters the constitution, a plebiscite does not. In England it was used pejoratively to describe the votes held by Napoleon to assert his authority, a foreshadowing of modern criticisms that autocrats use referendums to obtain a sheen of legitimacy.)

The peak of democracy

Switzerland is home to the most sophisticated system of direct democracy in the world. Its 5.5 million citizens of voting age are called upon to vote in referendums on average four times a year, on 10 to 15 topics. Recent subjects have included how to spend the income from road tax, banning some items of religious clothing or introducing a Universal Basic Income. A law that has just been passed by parliament can be challenged by a public vote if 50,000 signatures can be gathered (as happened with the government's Net Zero plans in 2021). Citizens can force an issue to be put to a nationwide vote on the basis of 100,000 signatures. Parliament has the power to propose an alternative to a citizens' initiative and then both options are put to a vote, with a third question asking which the electorate prefers. Switzerland only exists as a state at all because it was approved in a referendum of the cantons in 1848 and direct democracy was used to hold together a country made up of very strong regional and religious identities.

But there have been some twists in the tale. Direct democracy was suspended during the Second World War. Parliamentarians were sceptical about the return of the citizen-inspired referendum and they only resumed after the public voted in favour of it in 1949 – and even then only by a majority of 50.7 to 49.3 per cent. Popular votes in immigration have recently put the country on a collision course with the EU and international law. And this beacon of democracy only got round to giving women the vote in 1971.

Referendums have various triggers. They can be mandated by law, such as most changes to state constitutions in the United States. They can be launched by an administration as a political tool, as the British Conservative government did in 2016 with the vote on the United Kingdom's membership of the European Union. Or they can be triggered by citizens, in which case they are often referred to as 'initiatives'.

Ireland's referendums to introduce same-sex marriage in 2015 and to remove the constitutional ban on abortion in 2018 have been held up as models of good practice because the ground was laid with citizens' assemblies, information was widely accessible and minority views were shown respect. On the other hand, California's vote on Proposition 22 in 2020 – which asked whether ride-sharing apps such as Uber and Lyft should have to give their drivers full employment rights – showed the referendum used as a tool of elite politics as usual. The question was put on the ballot by the companies that owned the apps, not by a groundswell of public opinion. The campaign was waged by the established labour unions and big tech, who spent $224 million. There was an avalanche of misleading propaganda on both sides. And it led to three years of court hearings over whether the vote infringed the state legislature's power to regulate employment.

Deliberative democracy

The movement that seeks to make political decisions more inclusive and thoughtful is known as 'deliberative democracy', a phrase first coined by Stanford academic James Fishkin in a book in 1991. It includes the following techniques:

Deliberative polling, in which a random, representative sample of citizens is selected and surveyed about their opinion on a topic. They then spend a weekend receiving information and in intensive discussion on the subject, before being surveyed again to measure how their opinions have changed. Fishkin has suggested this could be turned into a nationwide public holiday, Deliberation Day.

Citizens' juries bring together small, representative groups of the population to chew over issues. The modern version of a very ancient Athenian-sounding idea was developed in the United States in the

1970s by the psychologist Ned Crosby and in Germany by Peter Dienel, who called them *Plannungszelle* or 'planning cells'.

Participatory budgeting gives citizens more say over how public money is spent by local authorities, combining a lot of mass meetings with systems for ranking priorities. Political scientists flocked to the southern port city of Porto Alegre in Brazil, where this approach was introduced on a large scale in 1989 by labour activists as a challenge to endemic corruption.

Critics of the deliberative approach cite the amount of time it requires. (Robert Dahl calculated that a meeting with 500 participants, where each spoke for 10 minutes, would take 10 days). Others query whether members of the public have enough knowledge to make wise decisions, whether direct democracy can overcome the age-old problem of minorities being outweighed by majorities or whether more discussion can really imbue decisions with greater legitimacy. In other words, new wrapper but the same old criticisms of democracy itself.

The condensed idea
The public make decisions directly

14 Social Democracy

Commenting on the living conditions of the working class in the north of England in the 1930s, in *The Road to Wigan Pier*, George Orwell wrote: 'To the ordinary working man, the sort you would meet in any pub on Saturday night, socialism does not mean much more than better wages and shorter hours and nobody bossing you about.' His beer-fuelled image nods to a version of a gentler, less ideological version of Marxism – social democracy. Mostly a product of western and northern Europe, there are parties that are Social Democrats. There are countries that are social democracies. And politicians who describe themselves as democratic socialists.

The German Social Democrats

The idea of a social democratic party developed in Germany in the late 19th century. The Social Democratic Party of Germany (SPD) formed in 1875 after a merger of the Social Democratic Workers' Party and the General German Workers' Union. Formally, the SPD stood on a Marxist platform. But in practice it moved away from the idea of socialism being introduced by revolutionary means and advocated the use of the democratic process instead. Despite being banned by German Chancellor Otto von Bismarck as a security threat, members of the party started winning seats in the German parliament, the Reichstag, becoming the largest group in 1912.

A leading intellectual influence in the SPD was Eduard Bernstein, the son of a train driver and former friend of Marx and Engels. He caused a big row in the party when he rejected its Marxist stance. He saw growing evidence that capitalism was working. The economy was growing, living conditions were improving. Capitalism could make people's lives better, not utterly miserable. And where there was misery, why not seek to mitigate it rather than destroy the entire system? This was captured in his book *Die Voraussetzungen des Sozialismus und die Aufgaben der Sozialdemokratie*. It had a snappier title in English: *Evolutionary Socialism*.

'We have to take working men as they are. And they are neither so universally pauperized as was set out in the Communist Manifesto, nor so free from prejudices and weaknesses as their courtiers wish to make us believe. They have the virtues and failings of the economic and social conditions under which they live.'

This pointed believers in socialism towards regulation of the economy, rather than a new type of society.

Towards the Golden Age

The social democratic tradition in the United Kingdom was embodied in the Fabian Society. Its power couple at the turn of the 20th century were the poverty researchers, campaigners and prolific hosts of intellectual dinner parties, Beatrice and Sidney Webb. In 1905 Beatrice was appointed to a committee reviewing Britain's Poor Law, under which workers received accommodation in return for their labour. The inquiry proposed some reforms, but Webb disagreed with the majority view on the committee and published her own Minority Report. In it she recommended cash payments for the poor and a unified public health service. The report was heavily promoted and widely discussed but its recommendations were rejected by the government of Herbert Asquith. The Webbs would instead join the socialist Labour Party in 1914 and help to write its constitution.

The election of the Labour government of Clement Attlee in the United Kingdom, in 1945, meant that Webb's ideas were finally put into practice, with the creation of the Welfare State. This was accompanied by a 'mixed' economy of both private and state-owned companies and a goal of full employment, supported by generous government spending, based on the ideas of the economist of John Maynard Keynes.

Meanwhile the Scandinavian countries had pioneered new ways to manage the relationship between the workers, companies and the state. For example, Swedish employers and unions signed the Saltsjöbaden Agreement in 1938, which introduced collective bargaining over wages and conditions for whole sectors of the economy and set out new rules about the right to strike.

This was the social democratic blueprint: good labour relations, a generous welfare system to ensure the needs of all citizens are met, paid for by high taxes and a growing economy under the stewardship of the state. It became the dominant model of government for so much of western Europe that the postwar period of 1945–75 is known as the Golden Age of Social Democracy.

The evolution of social democracy

The economic crises of the 1970s showed that economic growth was not endless and that there were limits to how far a government could manage the economy. The rise of right-wing economics and politics forced social democrats to change. This story is told by the evolution of the British Labour Party, even if it calls itself a 'democratic socialist' party rather than a truly social democratic party.

Confronted by a wave of strikes known as the Winter of Discontent, James Callaghan's Labour administration was thrown out and replaced by the Conservative government of Margaret Thatcher in 1979. Labour's response was to move further to the political left. A group of Labour MPs – the Gang of Four – resigned in 1981 to form the Social Democratic Party. They failed to break through electorally and later merged with the Liberal Party to form the Liberal Democrats. After three more election defeats, Tony Blair became the Labour leader in 1994. His trademark moment was his 1995 rewriting of Clause IV of the party's constitution, which had called for the state ownership of industry. Blair later explained:

'When drafted in 1917 . . . [Clause IV] reflected prevailing international progressive thought that saw the abolition of private capital as something devoutly to be desired. What was mainstream leftist thinking in the early 20th century had become hopelessly unreal, even surreal, in the late-20th-century world in which, since 1989, even Russia had embraced the market . . . No one believed in it, yet no one dared remove it.'

Labour's victory in the UK election of 1997 and the return of the Social Democrats to power in Germany at roughly the same time marked the late 1990s and early 2000s as a renaissance for social democracy, at least in its new form.

The crisis of social democracy?

After the Global Financial Crisis of 2007–09, social democratic parties started losing elections or flat-lining in the opinion polls – in the United Kingdom, France, Greece, Germany, Scandinavia. In his 2016 pamphlet *Social Democracy Without the Social Democrats*, the political commentator Neal Lawson summed up the potential causes: the mobility of capital meant that national governments lost some of their power, voters were turning to more nationalistic politics, and privatization meant there were fewer spaces in national life where social democracy could be practised. Plus, the practitioners themselves may have become a bit haughty for the modern world: 'The whole premise of the offer was, and is, that if you elect a social democratic government, it does things to you and for you, you are in turn grateful and therefore vote for them again.'

The condensed idea
Socialist-ish

15 Consensus Democracy

' Instead of being satisfied with narrow decision-making majorities, it seeks to maximize the size of these majorities. Its rules and institutions aim at broad participation in government and broad agreement on the policies that the government should pursue.' What's not to like about a consensus democracy? Also known as consociational democracy, it is a model identified by Dutch political theorist Arend Lijphart in his *Patterns of Democracy* – required reading for politics undergraduates. These are countries – often western European – where the watchwords are 'inclusiveness, bargaining and compromise'. A consensus democracy can help to manage the risk of conflict between diverse groups and lead to a better quality of democracy. Or so Lijphart's theory goes.

I heart Belgium

Lijphart plots ten variables that characterize a consensus democracy versus a majoritarian one and finds most of them present in Belgium. The country's location (between France, the Netherlands and Germany) and its history (fought over by France, the Netherlands and Germany) has created different communities, where tensions are smoothed over by a complex federal system with elements based on both geography and language. Belgium can seem baffling to outsiders, political scientists . . . and residents. The fact that it went for 652 days without a federal government in 2018–20 due to tortuous coalition negotiations has been interpreted as a sign of both the strength and the weakness of the system.

Forming a government in Belgium inevitably involves sharing power, Lijphart's first condition for a consensus democracy. The Belgian constitution mandates that jobs in the cabinet be split equally between politicians from the country's two main language communities, Dutch and French. The second condition is that there is give and take between parliament and the cabinet, and there is much more of that in Belgium than, say, the United Kingdom. The third and fourth conditions for a consensus democracy are a multi-party system and that elections are held proportionally, meaning that the outcome reflects the true number of votes cast, rather than alternative systems such as first past the post which can exaggerate a political party's success. Belgium ticks both these boxes, with the 150 seats of the House of Representatives usually occupied by more than 10 different parties.

The fifth condition is that there is strong cooperation between the state and interest groups, such as trade unions and business. Other academics say that trade union power probably peaked in Belgium in the 1960s. But Belgians can still feel remnants of this every day because healthcare and welfare benefits are organized less by the state and more by 'mutual' organizations based on liberal, socialist or Christian democratic traditions.

Lijphart's sixth requirement is a federal system where power is dispersed around the country. In Belgium this began happening on an epic scale from 1970. The largest administrative building blocks are based on geography: Flanders in the north, Wallonia in the south and Brussels-Capital in the centre. There are parliaments representing different languages – French, Dutch and German. Some of these units overlap, some do not. Public services are often delivered in a very devolved way, for example there are almost 200 local police forces in a country of fewer than 12 million people.

The seventh condition is that a country's parliament has two chambers and that both houses are matched in their powers. Condition number eight demands a written constitution that is fairly rigid – in other words, it requires a big effort to change it. Belgium adopted its document in 1832, with some fairly regular amendments. They require a two-thirds majority in both houses of parliament. And some alterations require a super-majority of both French and Dutch speakers, effectively giving a veto to either. The ninth and tenth conditions of consensual democracy are a strong court that can review the constitutionality of the government's actions and that there is an independent central bank that can oversee monetary policy. Belgium has both, although it got them pretty late.

Outcomes

Lijphart uses some impressive number-crunching to reach the conclusion that, on economic matters, consensual states might have the edge over their majoritarian rivals, but only just. Where these systems excel, he argues, is on 'kinder, gentler' politics – with more

From conflict to consensus

Consensual democracies are often created to heal societies after conflict, but two examples show there can be different outcomes.

The Belfast/Good Friday Agreement of 1998 was the culmination of the peace process to end The Troubles in Northern Ireland, the violence between Protestants and Catholics that cost the lives of more than 3,600 over three decades. The negotiations were a real-time attempt to build a consensus democracy within a contested system. Northern Ireland would remain a part of the United Kingdom as long as its people consented. Both the British and Irish governments gave up their claims. The deal created new institutions between the United Kingdom and Ireland and within Northern Ireland, including an elected Assembly.

The agreement specified how the Assembly and Northern Ireland's government, the Executive, would be formed, and how roles would be divided between Nationalists who looked towards Ireland and Unionists who looked towards the United Kingdom. The agreement allowed people in Northern Ireland to identify as British, Irish, Northern Irish or a combination of all three. Peace has broadly been maintained but regular political crises have required attention and occasional tweaks to the overall settlement, even if the text of the agreement has not changed. The 1998 deal was the middle of the peace process, not its beginning or end.

Since its formation in 1920, Lebanon operated under a system called 'confessionalism', where seats in the parliament were allocated proportionately based on the country's many different religious groups, which included six different branches of Christianity. The ratio of seats was 6:5 Christian to Muslim. The job of president was reserved for a Maronite Christian, the prime minister had to be Sunni and the speaker of parliament Shia. An agreement reached in Al-Ta'if in Saudi Arabi in 1989 to bring an end to Lebanon's multi-decade civil war was supposed to lead to reform of this arrangement. The introduction of proportional voting was also meant to bring in fairer representation. But the outcome has been paralysis of the Lebanese political system, making it difficult for the country to handle a wave of assassinations, protests, hyperinflation and a series of disasters, including forest fires and a huge explosion in Beirut's port – all while civil war has raged in neighbouring Syria.

generous welfare states, protection of the environment, family-friendly policies, the representation of women, and public participation in the electoral and governing process. Decisions reached by consensus can be just as decisive as those made by a government that wins a first-past-the-post election, he says in a challenge to believers in majoritarianism.

The condensed idea
Let's all try to get along

16 Pluralism

Pluralism has become a shorthand that connotes the vibrancy of a democracy. How many voices are heard? How many media outlets are there? How many issues are pushed by campaign groups? How much influence is granted to the opposition parties? And, in particular, how are different religious beliefs accommodated?

In politics, the word 'pluralism' originated in head-scratching debates in philosophy where concepts can comprise many things (pluralism) or just one (monism). Initially it was borrowed by British political thinkers whose goal was to shift power away from a coercive state and towards voluntary organizations, a process they dubbed 'pluralism'. Then pluralism morphed into a theory about the interaction of competing interest groups, which dominated American political science in the 1950s and 1960s, before it became the more general term in use now.

The dangers of factions

The idea that a diversity of views is a good thing for democracy was a big feature in *The Federalist* papers written by James Madison and others in the 1780s to promote the virtues of the new US Constitution to the American public. In *Federalist* paper no. 10, Madison warned that the biggest danger to the young republic was the emergence of 'factions' – groups based on common interests such as property ownership that were 'adversed to the rights of other citizens, or to the permanent and aggregate interests of the community'.

Because factions were a natural product of people having opinions, Madison argued that the only ways to prevent their formation was either by suppressing freedom or enforcing conformity. Neither of these were good. For Madison, it was better to limit the effects of factions instead. The way the United States would do this was through its size and federal structure. A big country would have more opinions. A big electorate would produce better representatives, who could 'refine and enlarge the public views'. A big federation would mean no state could dominate the others. In other words, diversity was strength. So the United States was founded on principles that could be called pluralist, even if the founders did not use the word.

British pluralists

The 20th century version of this was promoted by the British left-wing thinker Harold Laski. He left the United Kingdom for North America in 1914 after falling out with his Jewish family over his marriage to a Christian woman. At Harvard University, Laski formulated his theories of pluralism. He challenged the view that the state should have a monopoly on sovereignty. Instead, power should be decentralized and lie with groups where membership was voluntary, such as trade unions or churches.

Following the Great Depression and the rise of fascism in Europe, Laski returned to the United Kingdom, where he became more of a Marxist and focused on class relations. His language also became increasingly dramatic. Incidentally, as chair of the British Labour Party's National Executive Committee, Laski also received one the greatest put-downs in political history. During a damaging argument with the party leader Clement Attlee about who was in charge, Attlee wrote to Laski in 1945 and told him, 'A period of silence on your part would be welcome.'

> The structure of social organization involves, not myself and the state, my groups and the state, but all these and their interrelationships . . . The interest of the community is the total result of the whole pressure of social forces.
> Harold Laski

Who governs?

The idea that power was dispersed rather than wielded from the top down was expanded upon by the influential American academic Robert Dahl, including in his 1961 book *Who Governs?* Dahl spent two years immersed in the political life of the coastal Connecticut city of New Haven, then with a population of around 160,000. He interviewed 50 people in depth and surveyed hundreds. He studied decisions about urban redevelopment and schools, and every single nomination for political office. An associate was stationed in City Hall for a year as an observer and his students combed the archives. Dahl's conclusion was that decisions in New Haven were a product of endless bargaining and 'the steady appeasement of small groups'. Everyone had some power; no one had total control. Everyone had access to political resources – whether popularity, education, social status, the law or money – which they then spent in different ways. And the wealthy were not as power-obsessed as some people thought. 'One wealthy man may collect paintings; another may collect politicians,' Dahl wrote.

The answer Dahl gave to his question of 'Who governs?' was . . . 'No one.' From this he extrapolated his pluralist theory to the entire United States, to the economy, to issues of war and peace. The pluralist concept grew in popularity and came to dominate American political science, before coming under serious criticism in the 1960s and 1970s. Pluralists were accused of failing to acknowledge the extent to which some groups were excluded from the bargaining process or the power of dominant groups to exert control over it.

Measuring pluralism

Such is Canada's reputation as a pluralistic society that the leader of Shia Ismaili Muslims and philanthropist, the Aga Khan, set up his Global Centre for Pluralism in Ottawa in association with the Canadian government. It runs the rule over countries using 20 variables that include membership of international agreements promoting pluralism, public trust in institutions and government policies. It mainly interprets pluralism as the number of opportunities for minorities to influence national life. In their 2022 report on Canada, the country did spectacularly well on representation of citizens of the French-speaking province of Quebec and for foreign-born Canadians but the scores were much lower for indigenous people, often a lot lower. The report pointed out, for example, that provinces can veto changes to the Canadian constitution but indigenous communities cannot and that indigenous languages do not receive the same official protection as French and English.

Today's academic debate about pluralism encompasses politics, ethics, religion and philosophy. The philosopher John Gray made the complicated argument that pluralism killed off the idea of liberalism because liberalism requires that nothing other than liberalism exists, which means that pluralism cannot exist in liberalism. And the Belgian philosopher Chantal Mouffe maintained that pluralism meant strongly held differences were an inevitable part of society, and so politicians should abandon the idea of consensus and embrace never-ending argument. Then there are those who take the more lyrical view, as put by the late African American poet Maya Angelou: 'In diversity there is beauty and there is strength.'

The condensed idea
How power is spread

17 The European Union

The European Union (EU) is a club of 27 member countries who have agreed to implement shared laws, eliminate the borders between them, adopt a collective policy for trade with the rest of the world and, in some cases, share the same currency – the euro. The idea of 'ever closer union' came from the diplomatic salons of Paris after the Second World War, beginning with the Schuman Plan, signed in 1950. Foreign ministers and intellectuals sought to prevent future conflicts between France and Germany by fusing together the coal and steel industries of western Europe.

> The pooling of coal and steel production . . . will change the destinies of those regions that have long been devoted to the manufacture of munitions of war, of which they have been the most constant victims.
>
> Schuman Plan, May 1950

But these origins – elite and economic – have meant that the modern-day European Union has struggled to make a connection with its citizens who live in nation-states with clear identities of their own. This is called 'the democratic deficit'. The idea of a political project running ahead of the desires of voters was captured by the late Polish politician Bronislaw Geremek when he wrote: 'We have made Europe. Now we must make Europeans.'

Designed to be democratic

The two treaties that govern the functioning of the EU created institutions that are supposed to have democracy in their DNA. The European Council is made up of the *elected* heads of state and government of the member states. They make the big, strategic decisions at regular summits (and at emergency meetings during a crisis). Representatives in the European Parliament have been directly *elected* since 1979. The members of the European Commission, which proposes new laws and monitors existing policies across the EU, are appointed by their *elected* national governments. New laws must be agreed by all three institutions, a practice designed to encourage compromise. National parliaments in the individual member states then usually get to decide how initiatives are implemented in their domestic legal systems.

Voilà, c'est démocratique?

So what is the problem? The EU's legislative system is complicated and opaque. The final part of the process – when the council, parliament and commission haggle over the final wording of a new law – is called 'trilogue' and takes place in secret. Journalists tend to focus on whether their home country is winning or losing a policy battle rather than reporting on the content of the policy, which adds to the lack of scrutiny. Sometimes the EU has been accused of operating in a black box . . . literally. During trade negotiations with the United States, selected VIPs were invited into a sealed room to read the draft texts of the deals, which earned the ire of transparency campaigners.

Then there is the weirdness of the sittings of the European Parliament, which do not replicate the cut-and-thrust seen in many national assemblies. Proceedings are dominated by pre-prepared speeches and not genuine debate. Partly this is down to the language barrier and a desire to reduce confrontation. But it is also because the national political parties to which members of the European Parliament belong are also members of vast pan-European alliances of parties. These groups tend to stitch things up in advance so knife-edge votes are non-existent and there is rarely any political jeopardy worth tuning in for.

The lack of interest in this, the only directly elected institution in the European Union, is reflected in the turnout for the European Parliament elections. In Slovakia in 2014 it was 13 per cent. In 2019 it was 88 per cent of Belgians . . . and Belgium has compulsory voting. (The image of the European Parliament is not helped by it having two seats – one in Brussels, Belgium, and the other in Strasbourg, France. This requires a lot of expensive shuttling back and forth in planes, cars and even chartered trains.)

Within this system, it is easy for all the players to shift responsibility. The council can accuse the commission of being too bossy; the commission can insist it is following orders from prime ministers; the parliament can claim the will of the people is being ignored; and everyone can say they are only following rules laid down in treaties written years before, by politicians who left the stage long ago.

The constitution controversy

Sometimes the EU hands its critics a loaded gun. A proposed European Constitution was rejected by voters in France and the Netherlands in 2005, but much of its content came back in revised from with the Lisbon Treaty in 2007. Despite the EU's arguments that the treaty was substantially different and that national parliaments had the power to approve or veto it, the accusation stuck that the EU had ignored the wishes of its citizens. The United Kingdom's vote to leave the EU was partly a product of this. The Labour government failed to hold a promised vote on the Lisbon Treaty. Their Conservative successors pledged that they would put it to a referendum, which morphed into the UK's vote on whether to leave the EU altogether in 2016.

All of this causes genuine angst in Brussels and other EU capitals, and various attempts have been made to inject more democratic legitimacy. A recent example proves how difficult it is to deliver transnational democracy. Every few years the so-called 'top jobs' in the EU – the presidents of the council, commission, parliament and European Central Bank – have to be filled. The idea was that the pan-European political alliances would nominate a lead candidate – a *Spitzenkandidat* – to take over as head of the commission. The political family that won the most seats in the parliament would get the top job. For example, the centre-right parties that run collectively as the European People's Party presented the German MEP Manfred Weber as their front man. Who? That was the problem. Voters felt no connection to the candidates, and few were aware that this system was in operation. The bigger issue was that the prime ministers and presidents of the member states ignored the whole thing and just picked the people they wanted anyway. In secret.

As an alternative to trying to generate democratic legitimacy, the EU institutions have focused instead on promoting their usefulness to citizens in the modern era: the borderless Schengen Area, which means European citizens rarely have to show their passports when they travel within the EU, the single market of common regulations for goods, which cuts costs for businesses, and a large-scale response to big problems such as Covid and the Russian invasion of Ukraine. This strategy is inspired by the Schuman Plan, the founding document of the European integration project, which said: 'Europe will not be made all at once, or according to a single plan. It will be built through concrete achievements that first create a de facto solidarity.'

And there is a twist. The EU's opinion pollsters Eurobarometer found in winter 2022 that more voters had a positive attitude towards the European Union than their national governments: 47 per cent to 32 per cent. This suggests apathy about the EU institutions in Brussels rather than anger. It also might explain why no other countries followed the lead of the United Kingdom, which left the club in 2020. Despite fears at the time, the words Frexit or Italexit have not been added to the dictionary alongside Brexit.

The condensed idea
Europe's ever closer union

18 Indian Democracy

I ndia is the world's largest democracy. The outcomes of its elections matter for the world because the nation of 1.4 billion people is being wooed by the United States as part of its rivalry with China. Prime Minister Narendra Modi's promotion of Hindutva – 'Hinduness' – has stretched the constitutional commitment to secularism, affecting the lives of the roughly 20 per cent of the population who are members of other religions, and the country's relationship with its Muslim neighbour Pakistan. Some 912 million citizens were eligible to vote at the election in 2019, so the quality of India's elections and political system affect more people than in any other country.

A constitutional inheritance

Much of India's 146,000-word constitution was inherited from laws passed in Britain during colonial rule and so the country's political set-up resembles that of the United Kingdom. As at Westminster,

> We, the people of India having solemnly resolved to constitute India into a sovereign socialist secular democratic republic . . .
> Preamble to the Indian Constitution

there is a parliament with two chambers. The upper house, the Rajya Sabha (Council of States), is designed to represent the units of the Indian federal system – the 28 states and the 8 union territories that are run from Delhi. It is elected by members of the state legislatures and not directly by the public. It also includes 12 members chosen by the president from the worlds of art, literature and public service.

The directly elected lower chamber, the Lok Sabha (House of the People), is limited to 552 members. Each constituency elects a single representative under a British-style first-past-the-post system, where the winner is the candidate with the most votes (a plurality, not necessarily a majority). More than a hundred seats are reserved for the tribes and castes mentioned in the constitution. A constitutional amendment in 2019 abolished the two members who can be appointed by the president to represent the Anglo-Indian community. Like the British system, the largest party in parliament forms the government, which is led by a prime minister and supported by a cabinet of ministers.

For decades, power was held by the Indian National Congress (INC), led by descendants of the country's first prime minister, Jawaharlal Nehru. Since 2014, the Bharatiya Janata Party (BJP) has been the largest in parliament. It was the first party other than the INC to have formed a majority government. The BJP leader Narendra Modi has dominated Indian politics and played an increasingly influential role in politics across the globe.

A flawed democracy?

Advocates of a more proportional voting system point out that the number of seats won by the BJP in 2019 outweighed their share of the vote. A review of the size of electoral districts has been delayed by decades, meaning that the average constituency in Uttar Pradesh has half a million more voters than in less densely populated Kerala. In other words, the criticisms that are made of all first-past-the-post electoral systems.

The democracy-monitoring organization Freedom House also lists a litany of concerns about the conduct of Indian politics. They include the repression of journalists who are critical of the government and the prevalence of fake news. There has been a big increase in the use of the country's Unlawful Activities Prevention Act to raid non-governmental organizations and detain their members. The country's highest-profile opposition politician, Rahul Gandhi, was ejected from parliament after being found guilty of defamation, a charge widely believed to be politically motivated. This, while more than 40 per cent of candidates in the 2019 election had criminal records, according to the campaign group the Association for Democratic Reforms (ADR).

But the biggest criticisms centre around the treatment of religious minorities, especially Muslims. Thousands of people protested in several states in 2022 over a BJP spokesman's remarks about the prophet Muhammad, prompting a violent crackdown. A new national register of citizenship was criticized for disenfranchising Muslims when it was trialled in the state of Assam, which has a large Muslim population. The Supreme Court halted a programme of demolishing homes with Muslim owners. Dr Gareth Pierce of the Chatham House thinktank asked whether such 'a monochrome vision can fit in a country as diverse

Democracy at scale

Everything about India's parliamentary election in 2019 was big. Nearly 4 million voting machines were deployed to more than one million polling stations. Because of a rule that no voter should have to travel more than 2 km (1¼ miles) to cast their vote, polling places are set up on sandbars, in deserts, on glaciers. Two polling stations each serviced a single voter, one situated in a forest in Gujarat. Twelve million officials worked on delivering the election, which was split into seven phases, spread over two months. But this huge exercise ends with a small gesture for every voter – a semi-permanent dash of purple ink applied to the forefinger of their left hand by the polling clerk to show that they have exercised their right to vote.

Democracy was suspended between June 1975 and March 1977 in a period known as The Emergency. This was introduced by the Prime Minister Indira Gandhi, based on clause 352 of the constitution, which allowed her to delay the parliamentary elections and imprison opponents to deal with 'internal disturbances'. Announcing the state of emergency, she told the country: 'I am sure you are all conscious of the deep and widespread conspiracy that has been brewing ever since I began introducing certain progressive measures of benefit to the common man and woman of India in the name of democracy. It has sought to negate the very functioning of democracy.' Mrs Gandhi was assassinated by her Sikh bodyguards in the garden of her residence in 1984.

as India'. Yet polling conducted by the Pew Research Centre in 2020 found that roughly the same number of Hindus as Muslims reported experiencing 'a lot' of religious discrimination – 21 per cent to 24 per cent. An equal number – 65 per cent – from both communities said that communal violence was a very big national problem.

Speaking to journalists on a visit to the Oval Office in Summer 2023, Modi said he was 'surprised' about their criticisms of India's human rights' record. 'We have always proved that democracy can deliver. And when I say deliver, this is regardless of caste, creed, religion, gender.

There's absolutely no space for discrimination,' he added. His supporters point out that the BJP's dominance of national politics is not replicated at a local level. Modi also does not win every fight. For example, in 2021 he backed down in a year-long long dispute with farmers over reforms to Indian agriculture that saw thousands of tractors lining the roads to New Delhi. Nonetheless, in annual surveys India is labelled as 'an electoral autocracy', a 'hybrid regime' or 'a flawed democracy'.

The condensed idea
The world's largest democracy

19 Tyranny

I n 2015, political scientist Larry Diamond used the phrase 'democratic recession' to capture the trend that saw the number of democracies in the world declining – or at least, flatlining – after a big increase since the 1970s. This has led to a renewed focus on past and present types of government that are not democratic – absolute monarchy, dictatorship, autocracy, oligarchy. Based on different ideologies such as fascism, communism and nationalism, they remind us that non-democracies have been the norm for much of human history.

The tyrant

'Great is the honour bestowed on him who kills a tyrant,' wrote Aristotle in *Politics*, where he identified tyranny as the inverted form of monarchy, which was enlightened rule by a single person. 'This tyranny is just that arbitrary power of an individual which is responsible to no one, and governs all alike, whether equals or better, with a view to its own advantage, not to that of its subjects, and therefore against their will. No freeman willingly endures such a government.' Aristotle saw that tyrants focused on growing their own wealth and encouraged their people to do so too, because they would then be too busy for civic activities that could challenge the tyrant's power. A tyrant chipped away at the bonds of family, friendship and community and sowed division between groups. Aristotle believed tyrannies prevented people reaching their full potential, which contravened the laws of nature.

Despotism

The despot was another type of ruler identified by Aristotle. He saw them outside Greece in places such as Persia and the Byzantine Empire. Despotism was more like a master-slave relationship, and because the powerless had effectively consented to be ruled over by the powerful, it could therefore be regarded as just.

French theorist Charles-Louis de Secondat de Montesquieu expanded on the concept of despotism in the first half of the 18th century. In *De l'esprit des Lois* (The Spirit of Laws), published in 1748, he boiled down the types of state to three, each with its own distinct flavour: republics based on virtue, monarchies based on honour, and despotism based on fear. He was mainly criticizing the monarchies of Louis XIV and Louis XV, who had disempowered the institutions of French society, but he believed that any form of government could mutate into despotism, writing: 'Monarchy usually degenerates into the despotism of one; aristocracy into the despotism of several; democracy into the despotism of the people.'

Despotism could take different forms. It could make life 'like that of beasts' and be characterized by 'instinct, compliance and punishment', or it could result in a population that was quite rich and happy because they had been encouraged to be so as a distraction by their 'lazy, voluptuous and ignorant' ruler. The tendency towards despotism proved, for Montesquieu, why the separation of powers was necessary. Spreading authority between an executive, legislature and judiciary acted as a guard against any system's potential slide towards over-mightiness. These ideas were influential in the American and French revolutions.

(With Montesquieu's references to Ottoman sultans, their wives and eunuchs, nowadays there is a whiff of xenophobia around much of this type of thinking about despotism because it was based on a particular view of how things worked outside western Europe.)

Fascism

The *fasces* was a bundle of reeds with an axe head attached, carried in ancient Rome as a symbol of authority. It was adopted in name and image when Benito Mussolini formed his National Fascist Party in Italy in 1921. The fascist regimes that spread around the world, but mostly in Europe, during the 20th century varied by country but all tended to rally their supporters around narratives of national decline, racial superiority and the personality of the leader.

The academic Robert Paxton, in his *Anatomy of Fascism*, adds 'a compensatory cult of unity, energy and purity, in which a mass-based party of committed nationalist militants, working with uneasy but effective collaboration with traditional elites, abandons democratic liberties and pursues with redemptive violence and without ethical or legal restraints goals of internal cleansing and external expansion'. He elaborates five stages in a fascist party's arc: creation, taking root in the political system, seizure of power, exercise of power and, finally, 'entropy'.

Totalitarianism

During the 20th century, Nazi Germany and the Soviet Union gave the world terrible lessons in modern forms of tyranny. Few people chronicled this as vividly as the Jewish journalist and author Hannah Arendt, who fled Europe in 1941 and settled in the United States where she wrote *The Origins of Totalitarianism* (1953). Totalitarianism for Arendt meant the control of everything in a society by a leader. And she meant *everything* – a person's friendships, their family, even their thoughts and perceptions.

> 'What totalitarian ideologies aim at is not the transformation of the outside world or the revolutionizing transmutation of society, but the transformation of human nature itself.'
>
> Hannah Arendt,
> *The Origins of Totalitarianism*

This was achieved by destroying relationships and eliminating individuality in order to create a single 'mass' of lonely, isolated individuals who could be manipulated. Stalin did this by 'liquidating' the peasantry, property owners and the people who ran factories or businesses. Propaganda used lies to create an alternative reality. A totalitarian organization of officials and secret police maintained order, ruthlessly. The result was that human beings became 'superfluous' and so could be killed in vast numbers. Hitler did this in the concentration camps, Stalin in his purges and manufactured famines.

Authoritarianism and dictatorship

Scholars contrast totalitarian with authoritarian regimes where there is less control over private life and maybe a little bit more tolerance of dissent . . . but not much. Arendt herself says the Soviet Union became less totalitarian after the death of Stalin. She also made a distinction between totalitarians and *dictators*. The former terrorized everyone, whereas the latter tended to focus on their political opponents. Dictatorship has its origins in the Roman Republic. To the Romans, this meant an official taking on sweeping powers to handle an emergency, but the arrangement would be temporary and subject to approval and veto by others in the system.

Oligarchy

In Aristotle's influential typology of governments, an *oligarchia* is led by a group of people for their benefit. It is the negative form of an aristocracy. In the 1990s, a class of super-rich oligarchs emerged in Russia, with the privatization of Soviet state assets. There is debate about the level of political influence they wield nowadays, despite Russia frequently being described as an oligarchy. In 2023 US Democratic Senator Bernie Sanders said: 'Of course the oligarchs run Russia.' He added: 'But guess what? Oligarchs run the United States as well . . . And it's not just the United States, it's not just Russia; Europe, the UK, all over the world, we're seeing a small number of incredibly wealthy people running things in their favour.' A country run by a particularly wealthy elite is called a plutocracy. A kleptocracy – literally rule by thieves – is when leaders or elites use their country's resources to enrich themselves.

Literary tyrants

A literary take on tyranny became famous when the then German Chancellor Angela Merkel chose it as her holiday reading. Her book of choice was Harvard Professor Stephen Greenblatt's *Tyrant*, a study of authoritarian leaders in Shakespeare's plays. Through its examination of Coriolanus, Macbeth and Richard III, among others, Greenblatt investigates how the playwright made these characters simultaneously hateful and likeable, how they frequently promised to make their countries 'great again' and how they were enabled by courtiers who believed their leader's worst impulses could be tamed. Another theme was that Shakespeare avoided political trouble by using historical examples to comment on current controversies. Written in 2018, Greenblatt's book did not mention Donald Trump once.

The condensed idea
Some rule is rotten

20 Anarchism

What defines anarchism? Is an anarchist the anti-capitalist protestor playing bongo drums peacefully in front of police outside a bank, for example? Or is it an anti-capitalist protestor chucking firebombs violently at police outside a bank? Or perhaps the true anarchist is the person who rejected capitalism by living in a shack in the woods? The answer is that all three are anarchists, because anarchists differ widely from each other in their methods and goals, and in their conception of human nature: are we selfish or collaborative, tending to be good, tending to be bad, ready to be corrupted or waiting to be improved? All this becomes clear in the history of anarchist thought, which is much richer than the clichéd images suggest.

The sharper men's weapons

The general idea behind anarchism is that allowing yourself to be ruled goes against human nature. The state is a bad thing because it can only survive through coercion. This concept has existed for a long time and has been expressed in various forms, including in religions that include Daoism in China.

> The more laws and restrictions,
> the poorer people become.
> The sharper men's weapons,
> the more trouble in the land.
> The more ingenious and clever men,
> the more strange things happen.'
>
> Daoist poem, China, 400 BCE

Ideas that sounded very anarchist were put forward by Gerrard Winstanley during the English Civil War of 1642–51. Winstanley was a member of the Diggers, a group that created a collectivist community to jointly farm land on a hillside in Surrey in southern England. He argued that power and property were inherently corrupt. Later, in 1793, the English philosopher William Godwin made similar points in his work *Political Justice,* when he imagined a society based on small units and a barter economy. Neither of these men described themselves as an 'anarchist' and during these periods the label was instead used pejoratively to criticize revolutionaries, recalling the ancient Greek word *anarchos,* meaning 'without authority'.

Defining anarchy

The first person to identify as an anarchist – and proudly so – was the French politician Pierre-Joseph Proudhon. In the 1840s, after yet another failed revolution in France, with the monarchy re-established and the rich getting richer again, he came to his famous conclusion 'property is theft'. His solution was collective ownership and he felt that this could be achieved within society as it currently existed.

Around the same time, in the United States, Henry David Thoreau spent a blissful year or so living in a log cabin and concluded that everyone should basically do the same. He rebooted anarchism as a quiet, pastoral way of life.

Meanwhile, in Russia, the concept of common ownership but by revolutionary means was being cooked up by Mikhail Bakunin, who was first a friend – and then a fierce enemy – of Karl Marx. His theories were built upon by another Russian, Prince Peter Kropotkin, who rejected Charles Darwin's idea that nature was dominated by the survival of the fittest. Instead, Kropotkin saw that the natural world was full of examples of cooperation, which he described as 'mutual aid'. In his 1902 book, *Mutual Aid: A Factor of Evolution*, Kropotkin sang the praises of the British lifeboat service, the RNLI, whose volunteers sacrificed their time and potentially their lives to rescue those in trouble at sea.

Anarchisms

In the late 19th and early 20th centuries, anarchists pursued different means to achieve their varying visions of society. 'Anarcho-communists' believed in autonomous, self-governing communities where property was commonly owned. 'Anarcho-syndicalists' believed society should be organized on the basis of local trade unions. 'Anarcho-capitalists' believed in intense economic competition in a free market. Again, the thing they all had in common was the power of relations between individuals – a horizontal society, not a vertical one.

This sometimes took the form of anarchist violence, like the activists who bombed the Café Terminus in France in 1894 or assassinated US President William McKinley in 1901. The biggest experiment in living in an anarchist way was in eastern Spain in 1936, during the first few months of the Spanish Civil War.

Anarchism is not the same as libertarianism because libertarians usually accept that the state is necessary. They believe that the government's role should be minimized so that the individual's control of their own life can be maximized. Libertarianism has been a part of liberal thinking for centuries but received a modern boost in the work of the American philosopher Robert Nozick. In the 1970s he proposed the idea of the 'nightwatchman' state which guarantees the safety of its citizens but not much more. People had an inviolable right to own property which meant taxes, for Nozick, were 'on a par with forced labour'.

Crypto-currencies are a good example of libertarianism in practice. They are created by digital entrepreneurs and traded across borders in a pure free market. Their use is shaped by the users and morphs spontaneously. But numerous cases of fraud and yo-yoing values have led to calls for governments to regulate them. So crypto-currencies are unlikely to embody the libertarian dream for long.

Millions of people formed communes, where the ownership of the land and railways was collective and money was abolished – alongside coffee, strangely. General Franco's victory in the civil war brought that experiment to an end, and anarchism as a force declined elsewhere too.

Occupy Wall Street

A modern equivalent was the anti-capitalist Occupy movement, which began in Zuccotti Park in New York, near the financial institutions of Wall Street in 2011. Its in-house philosopher was David Graeber, an American who taught in the United Kingdom. He was co-author of the slogan 'We are the 99%'. In a blog post for the broadcaster Al Jazeera, he laid out the four ways in which the tented cities that popped up in more than a thousand actual cities around the world reflected the anarchist tradition:

1) Refusal to recognize the legitimacy of existing political institutions. Occupy never issued a list of demands because doing so would accept the demand for a list of demands from those in the existing structure, whether politicians or journalists. The movement just behaved in the way it wished the world was.

2) Refusal to accept the legitimacy of the existing legal order. Occupying a park in New York in such numbers was illegal, but surely public space belongs to . . . the public?

3) Rejecting an internal hierarchy in favour of consensus-based democracy. Occupy had no leaders (so noone could be bought off by the establishment) and decisions had to receive the approval of everyone (so there was no tyranny of the majority).

4) 'Pre-figurative politics' were embraced. Occupy did not just put up a bunch of tents, it also established libraries, kitchens and clinics in Kropotkin's spirit of mutual aid. This was another way of living the change they wanted.

Graeber died before his 60th birthday and Occupy Wall Street was moved on after 59 days, but in those four points it gives us a neat summary of a vein of historical thinking about democracy that is so much more than the bongos and firebombs imagery of anarchism.

The condensed idea
Pure freedom

21 China

I s China a model of 'political capitalism', where the Communist Party and the all-powerful President Xi Jinping steer a booming economy? Or is it a 'closed autocracy', with neither elections nor free media? Is China a 'political meritocracy', where there is intense competition among officials to rise to the top? Is it a perpetrator of genocide and torture? A 'systemic rival' or an ally in a partnership with 'no limits'? China has been described as each of these things by a Serbian-American economist, the V-Dem democracy monitoring project, a Canadian academic based in Beijing, human rights charities, the US government and the Kremlin, respectively.

A democratic turning point?

In its 2021 report, 'the China challenge', the Economist Intelligence Unit summed up the bargain between the Chinese and their government as 'a de facto social contract between the state and the people, in which the state is expected to deliver economic growth and raise living standards.'

For a few months in 1989, the Chinese elite argued over what this relationship should be. On the liberal wing, in opposition to the hard-liners, was the former General Secretary of the Chinese Communist Party, Hu Yaobang. He died of a heart attack and on the day of his funeral thousands of students and others gathered in Beijing's Tiananmen Square to demand democratic reforms. They erected a statue they called the Goddess of Democracy. The world was watching this proto-revolution because so many foreign journalists were in town to cover a visit by the Soviet leader Mikhail Gorbachev, marking a thaw in relations between former communist foes. Authorities dithered over their response to the protests before sending in troops to crush the movement at the beginning of June.

The 5 June was the day on which the 'Tank Man' photo was taken. To some the image of the unknown shopper facing down a line of tanks while carrying bags of groceries is the ultimate symbol of defiance. To others it is a misleading representation of restraint by the Chinese military, who killed many protestors elsewhere in the square and the city. The authorities claimed that there were 200 deaths. A telegram from a British diplomat that was declassified decades later suggested there were 10,000. Through censorship of the media, academia and the internet, the events of Tiananmen Square have been effectively erased from history by the Chinese government. The remaining memorial to the movement, which was in Hong Kong, has been removed.

Hong Kong

The former British colony has been the site of the most visible modern challenge to Communist Party authority. When the United Kingdom returned Hong Kong to the Chinese in 1997, there were fears about the consequences for democracy in the city. To provide reassurance, the Chinese government pledged to operate 'one country, two systems' and the handover agreement with the British specified that 'Rights and freedoms, including those of the person, of speech, of the press, of assembly, of association, of travel, of movement, of correspondence, of strike, of choice of occupation, of academic research and of religious belief will be ensured by law.'

But the Chinese have cracked down on those freedoms, meeting passionate resistance from pro-democracy activists. Attempts to reform the elections for the city's leader, the Chief Executive, led to 79 days of demonstrations at the end of 2014. The movement was named after the umbrellas used by protestors to defend themselves from tear gas and rubber bullets.

The biggest protests Hong Kong had ever seen – involving around 2 million people – were staged five years later, when a new law sought to ease extradition to the mainland. The proposal was dropped. But activists failed to prevent the introduction of the National Security Law (NSL) in June 2020, which criminalized most dissent. It led to thousands of arrests and the closure of the well-known newspaper *Apple Daily*. Several opponents of the NSL fled the city. In the summer of 2023 the authorities offered bounties for their capture of HK$1 million (around US$127,000). In Britain, parliamentarians concluded that China was operating 'One country, one system' and the government said the Sino-British Agreement had been breached.

China v the world

The crackdown on the democracy protests in Hong Kong contributed to record levels of immigration to its old colonial master, the United

Kingdom. The British government offered sanctuary to holders of British Nationals (Overseas) passports, a type of citizenship that was a legacy of the 1997 handover. There were 160,700 applications for visas in the first two years following the launch of the scheme, in January 2021, second only to the number of Ukrainians who arrived via humanitarian routes following invasion by Russia.

A lot of the world's disinformation is of Chinese origin. Journalists found the government pays money for social media posts to a '50-cent army', although researchers found that this was mostly state employees earning extra cash. A report by the Internet Institute at Oxford University detailed the activities of the pro-China 'little pink' cyber warriors, named after the colour of the forum where they organize. During the Covid pandemic, the European Union called out Chinese attempts to amplify conspiracy theories that the virus was spread by the United States. But there have also been signs of cyber-restraint by the Chinese government. It took down an independent troll army called Network Navy in 2018 and its network of aggressive diplomats – nicknamed 'wolf warriors' – seems to have toned down its online

Online control

Despite predictions that the internet would prove too unruly to control, the Chinese government has successfully continued its policy of online censorship. This has led to a game of cat and mouse where censors have to catch up with users, who post pictures of Winnie the Pooh as a proxy for Xi Jinping or of frogs to refer to the bespectacled former president Jiang Zemin.

There is widespread confusion among foreign observers around China's 'social credit' policy. Reports suggest this is a centralized system that links people's apps, finances and their behaviour to generate a score for good (or bad) citizenship. In reality, academics say, this is a messy combination of credit scores, regional experiments and regular features of apps, and that the Chinese government has plenty of existing tools to encourage compliance among the population.

rhetoric. Some academics believe China has decided to favour targeted campaigns against Taiwan and Tibet, and the prevention of dissent at home, rather than sowing chaos globally.

China dominates the foreign policies of many countries, whether they are the recipients of expensive loans from its enormous international infrastructure initiative, Belt and Road (Armenia, Kazakhstan, Laos, Kenya and numerous others), or as antagonists (the United States, Australia). A recurring feature has been misplaced optimism that engagement will lead to changes in the Chinese political system. A classic example is the speech by US President Bill Clinton in March 2000 after he had negotiated China's entry to the World Trade Organization: 'China is a one-party state that does not tolerate opposition. It does deny citizens fundamental rights of free speech and religious expression . . . But the question is not whether we approve or disapprove of China's practices. The question is, what's the smartest thing to do to improve these practices?' Yet many countries have also found themselves relying on Chinese investment and technology, such as 5G mobile phones and solar panels, which has caused conflict among China's rivals.

The condensed idea
Very big, not very democratic

22 Illiberal Democracy

Aristotle's pairs of constitutional types – monarchy/tyranny, aristocracy/oligarchy and polity/democracy – were joined by another in the late 1990s. It was liberal democracy's twin – 'illiberal democracy'.

The origins

The phrase was first used in 1997, by the Indian American journalist Fareed Zakaria, who would become a well-known anchor for the cable news channel CNN. He used the phrase in an article for the journal he edited, *Foreign Affairs*. The piece opened with a quotation from the American diplomat Richard Holbrooke about the first elections in newly democratic Bosnia in 1996. 'Suppose the election was declared free and fair,' Holbrooke is quoted as saying, but imagine those elected are 'racists, fascists, separatists, who are publicly opposed to [peace and integration]. That is the dilemma.'

Zakaria saw this happening across the world – in Peru, Pakistan, the Philippines, Slovakia. Yes, there were more democracies, but there were also more democratically elected leaders who were failing to uphold what Zakaria labelled 'constitutional liberalism' – the bundle of rights and institutions that provided for economic, religious and personal freedom and the protection of minorities. At the same time, unelected leaders were turning out to be better promoters of free markets and freedom of expression, showing the value of a sort-of liberal autocracy. Elections did not lead to liberal democracies; the link between liberalism and democracy had been broken. And perhaps that linkage was a fairly recent invention anyway, Zakaria argued, because for most of history liberals had wanted to constrain the power of the public.

This argument was challenged in the pages of *Foreign Affairs* a year later by Marc Plattner, the co-founder of the International Forum for Democratic Studies. 'Liberalism did not originally insist on democracy as a form of government, but it unequivocally insisted upon the ultimate sovereignty of the people,' he wrote. In other words, liberalism and sovereignty in the 19th century had not meant elections but the spread of universal suffrage in the 20th century meant that they now did. Nonetheless, Zakaria had punctured the euphoria about the spread of democracy after the collapse of the Soviet Union. He had also provided inspiration for a future European leader.

An illiberal democrat?

Hungarian Prime Minister Viktor Orbán took the phrase 'illiberal democracy' out of the pages of academic publications and adopted it as his governing philosophy. This put him on a collision course with the European Union, which very much prefers the liberal version. Orbán used Zakaria's formulation in a speech to his Fidesz party's summer camp in the lakeside town of Baile Tusnad in 2014. Taking inspiration from China, India, Turkey and Russia, Orbán set out his ambition to make Hungary an 'illiberal state'.

In a speech that has become notorious, Orbán took aim at liberalism as a doctrine of economics, cultural values and international politics. Economically, because Hungarians had become poorer at the hands of foreign-owned banks. Culturally, because Hungary's Christian identity had been undermined. Internationally, because EU funds to Hungary were administered by European bureaucrats paid vastly more than the average Hungarian.

Liberal values had become synonymous with 'corruption, sex and violence,' Orbán claimed in the 2014 speech. Even the free-market-obsessed United States had rejected the neo-liberal economic consensus in the wake of the global financial crisis, he told the crowd. Referring to the four years he had already been in office and looking forward to many more, he said:

> 'We needed to courageously state a sentence, a sentence that . . . was considered to be a sacrilege in the liberal world order. We needed to state that a democracy is not necessarily liberal. Just because something is not liberal, it still can be a democracy. Moreover, it could be and needed to be expressed, that probably societies founded upon the principle of the liberal way to organize a state will not be able to sustain their world competitiveness in the following years, and more likely they will suffer a setback, unless they will be able to substantially reform themselves.'

In practice, illiberal democracy Hungarian-style meant amending the constitution to define marriage as between a man and a woman only, outlawing the teaching of homosexuality in schools, refusing to accept refugees relocated from other EU countries, and occupying the diplomatic middle ground between the West and Russia during the invasion of Ukraine.

Orbán's critics at home and abroad argue that in his thirst to take the 'liberal' out of liberal democracy, he has also weakened the democracy. Reforms to the judiciary that gave the government more influence have been condemned regularly by the Venice Commission, which monitors the legal systems of countries that have signed the European Convention of Human Rights. Organizations that receive foreign funding – from charities to universities – have found it more difficult to operate. (A frequent target is the Hungarian-born billionaire and philanthropist George Soros, who paid for a younger, more liberal Viktor Orbán to study at Oxford University in 1989.)

Orbán and his allies argue that they have defended Hungarian values from assault by 'political activists paid by foreigners' and that they have four successive election victories to prove how popular this is. On the other hand, the election monitoring organization, the OSCE, assessed that the 2022 parliamentary elections were not fought on 'a level playing field'. The watchdog found that opposition candidates got little airtime in the media, which was dominated by government-supporting TV and radio stations, for example.

Challenging illiberal democracy

This has posed a big headache for the European Union, which counts Hungary as a member. In 2018 the European Parliament voted that Hungary was failing to respect democracy and the rule of law – the most basic criteria for being in the club. This process, known as Article 7 for the part of the EU treaty that talks about democracy in EU countries, went nowhere because enough other EU members, such as Poland, were doing the same thing. But poorer EU nations receive billions of euros in development funding from the richer ones. Officials have found ways to link that cash to the behaviour of the recipient countries. Money talks. Unless this makes Hungarian voters even angrier with liberal democratic international institutions, which would suit . . . Viktor Orbán.

To escape the binary divisions of liberal or illiberal, democratic or autocratic, political scientists use the phrase 'hybrid regime' as an umbrella term for countries that have a mixture of all of these elements. Within this category there are a huge number of variations: guided democracies (where there are elections, but policies do not change), anocratic regimes (dictatorships with apparently democratically elected legislature) or low intensity democracies (where other institutions, such as the military, hold more sway than the voting public.)

The Harvard University expert on populism Pippa Norris summarized the repressive components that are combined in different combinations in these systems as: 'weak checks and balances on executive powers, flawed or even suspended elections, fragmented opposition forces, state restrictions on media freedoms, intellectuals, and civil society organizations, curbs on the independence of the judiciary and disregard for rule of law, the abuse of human rights by the security forces, and tolerance of authoritarian values.'

In his 2021 book *Popular Dictatorships*, the Macedonian academic Aleksandar Matovski argued that the current generation of illiberal leaders embraced the democratic process to give themselves legitimacy, rather than repressing it to stay in power. In other words, rather than having illiberal democracy imposed on them, the people had voted for it.

The condensed idea
It's democracy, but not as we know it

23 Government

In a news conference in Illinois, in August 1986, about the struggles of American farmers, President Ronald Reagan made his famous quip that the nine most terrifying words in the English language were: 'I'm from the government and I'm here to help'. (Ironically, he then announced more government help for agriculture, proving that wanting a smaller state is not the same as delivering it.)

What is 'the government'? In the classic separation of powers model in which Reagan served, it is the 'executive' – which executes the laws that have been passed by the 'legislature' and are interpreted by the 'judiciary'. In the United States and much of Latin America, executive authority rests in a single person, the president. To the 19th-century revolutionary Simón Bolívar this made the chosen one 'an elected king in the name of president'.

Parliamentary government

In a parliamentary system such as in Australia or the United Kingdom, power is shared between the legislature and the executive. A cabinet of parliamentarians is appointed as ministers to run government departments and is led by a prime minister who is 'first among equals'. Under the policy of collective responsibility, ministers are allowed to

Cabinet curiosities

How a British cabinet functions is a combination of politics, and the prime minister's authority and personality. The Labour Party's Tony Blair had so much power that he could make decisions with such a small group of advisors that his style was nicknamed 'sofa government'. Conversely, the Conservative Theresa May was hamstrung by having to balance her cabinet between supporters and opponents of the United Kingdom's departure from the European Union (EU) and the loss of her party's majority in parliament. In Europe, a 'cabinet' usually refers to a leader's or minister's group of closest advisers.

fight like rats in a sack to defend the interests of their departments, then have to suppress their personal opinions once a decision has been adopted.

A focus on those at the top misses out many of the other elements that comprise the government of a modern liberal democracy, such as the permanent civil service. In 2020 government employees accounted for 30 per cent of all the jobs in Norway but just 12 per cent in the Netherlands, according to the EU statistical agency Eurostat. But international comparisons of the size of the government payroll can be misleading because some countries include the military and healthcare workers – groups that may or may not feel like part of the government depending on where you live. And then there are other public bodies that perform government-like functions. In the United Kingdom, these are called 'quangos'– quasi-autonomous non-governmental organizations.

Another tool to conceive of the power of a government is the amount of spending it does as a share of the country's economy. In 2021, this ranged from 24 per cent of Ireland's economy, to 44.9 per cent in the United States and 59 per cent in France, according to the think-tank for wealthy nations, the Organisation for Economic Co-operation and Development (OECD). Increased spending on defence in the wake of Russia's invasion of Ukraine and on pensions for an aging society, combined with repaying long-term debt from the Covid pandemic suggest these numbers will grow in the coming decades.

The purpose of government

A different way analysing governments is through grand theories – old and modern – about their purpose.

Bureaucracy The French philosopher Vincent de Gournay put the word *bureau* – writing desk – together with *-cratie* – meaning government – eventually leading to the word 'bureaucracy', the term used to describe the group of officials created under the reign of Louis XIV to administer France in the years before the French Revolution. The modern idea of a bureaucracy was defined by the German sociologist Max Weber. He argued that government by an organization of dispassionate professionals who were promoted on merit rather than wealth or privilege was a better way to run society than any other, such as feudalism or aristocracy. The bureaucracy administers the country on the basis of rules and procedures. Seeing the operation of government as the interplay between elements of the bureaucracy – government departments, office holders, service providers – can make the whole edifice seem a bit less confusing. The risk, for Weber, was that this system turned society into 'an iron cage'. This lies behind thousands of pejorative references to joyless bureaucrats.

Regulatory The theory of the 'regulatory state' holds that in the heyday of liberalism in the 18th and 19th centuries, there was little role for government because individuals and businesses were to be given maximum autonomy. This shifted into an era of bigger government, which began when the German Chancellor Otto von Bismarck introduced the first state pensions in the 1880s. This accelerated during the 'progressive era' in the early 20th century United States, when the state became more active in the control of companies and industry, and introduced big spending programmes, such as Roosevelt's New Deal. In the United Kingdom, the government took over the provision of services such as health and the railways, and developed the welfare state. The trend reversed in the 1970s and 1980s when politicians fell under the influence of the Chicago School of economists, who preached policies of deregulation and privatization, with much less state provision. But the private companies that now delivered public services such as water and energy had to be supervised to protect the interests of the citizens who relied on them, so regulatory agencies were created. Then, crises such as the financial crash of 2008, required even more state oversight. Under this theory, governments are now regulators of regulators and they 'steer rather than row' in the words of the political scientists David Osborne and Ted Gaebler.

Entrepreneurial The Italian-American-British economist Mariana Mazzucato has advocated that governments should act like entrepreneurs, backing new ideas and funding the development of technology where there is a high risk of failure. Her theory is that the state has historically been responsible for more innovation than the private sector. The most quoted chapter of her influential book *The Entrepreneurial State* explains that the iPhone only exists because government-sponsored labs invented touchscreens, GPS, voice recognition and the internet. She has recommended that governments organize themselves around big projects – 'moon shots' – that could benefit humanity, such as the development of new forms of green energy. This has earned her roles advising administrations in Italy, the United Kingdom, Sweden and a good number of international organizations.

Governance

The term 'governance' has taken on many meanings beyond a description of the actions of individual governments. It has become a by-word for the quality of a country's administration. Every year the World Bank publishes its World Governance Indicators, which judge countries on six measures: voice and accountability, political stability/the absence of terrorism, government effectiveness, quality of regulation, the rule of law and control of corruption. The organization has refuted criticisms that its data is biased because some of it comes from financial institutions, such as credit-rating agencies, or that its measures are too crude. The French philosopher Michel Foucault used the term 'governmentality' to describe the idea that citizens consent to being governed, which creates a relationship between them and meant 'government' was more than just another word for 'the state'.

The condensed idea
Running the country

24 Legislatures

T he term 'parliament' comes from the Norman French *parler*, meaning 'to speak'. The world's parliaments and their chambers have many names: the Commons, the House of Representatives, the Senate, the National Assembly, the Chamber of Deputies, the Duma. Broadly they are assemblies where representatives gather to scrutinize the government and to act as legislators, lawmakers. And these bodies vary in size, from seven members in the Shire Council of the Territory of Cocos to almost three thousand in the National People's Congress of China and around 1,500 in the United Kingdom's houses of Commons and Lords.

Icelandic origins

Iceland's parliament, the Althing, claims to be the world's oldest. Established in 930, it was a national version of the assemblies, *tings*, used by the Vikings to decide local issues. On a rocky outcrop known as *Lögberg* (the Law Rock) and under the chairmanship of the *lögsögumaður* (the Law Giver) laws were approved and legal battles fought.

The American scholar of Scandinavian languages Richard Beck reconstructed a sitting of the Althing in 1929: 'Socially it was the great event of the year. Leading men from all over the country met there, often bringing their wives and daughters as well as their retainers. Merchants returning from abroad hastened thither, bringing news no less than goods for sale. Athletes showed their prowess in various sports. Poets and story tellers entertained with their art. Invitations were exchanged and banquets held.'

Icelanders are proud of their stake in world parliamentary history but later colonial rule by Norway and then Denmark stripped the Althing of most of its powers. For centuries it functioned as a national court rather than a legislature and today's Althing is a modern invention from the 19th century.

The mother of parliaments

England was named as the 'mother of parliaments' by democracy campaigner John Bright in a speech in 1865. The origins of the British legislature lay in the agreement made between King John and the barons at Runnymede in 1215 that taxes could only be raised with the approval of wealthy landowners. In 1258, at a meeting in Oxford, the Earl of Leicester, Simon de Montfort, compelled John's son Henry III to share power with a council of advisors that would gather at the royal palace in Westminster. This evolved over centuries into the elected House of Commons and the appointed House of Lords (which includes some members who have inherited their positions from their fathers). The 'mother of parliaments' label ended up being attached less to England and more to its legislature as variations of the so-called 'Westminster model' were exported to Britain's colonies. Recently academics at University College London's Constitution Unit recommended the 'Westminster model' label be retired from international use because it risked 'trapping' institutions that had evolved their own conventions in 'a colonial past'.

There were 190 parliaments around the world in 2020, according to the Inter-Parliamentary Union, the organization that promotes representative institutions. That means 190 different sets of responsibilities, procedures and histories. But there are some broad ways to analyse them.

How many chambers?

A legislature that has one chamber is 'unicameral'; two is 'bicameral'. The second chamber can provide democratic checks and balances on another chamber that is dominated by one political party. It can revise and reflect on laws from different perspectives. It might also be a historical holdover from an era when monarchs, the Church and landowners ran the show. The United Kingdom's House of Lords combines all three. Sometimes the upper house exists to provide representation for different units of the constitutional set-up, such as the states in a federal system (the US Senate) or for ethnic groups (the House of Chiefs in Botswana). Popular perceptions of second chambers tend to be based on a combination of whether they are appointed or elected, strong or weak, a source of wisdom or politics as usual.

Does parliament provide the government?

Under 'parliamentarianism' the government, its leader and its ministers are provided by parliament. In other words, a party wins an election and becomes the majority in the legislature. It chooses a prime minister, who serves as long as he or she maintains the support of the majority in the parliament. This system does not have the clear separation of powers between the legislature and the executive that exists in presidential systems. Depending on your point of view, parliamentarianism is either more democratic because it gives the parliament power over the leadership, or less democratic because it turns parliament into the plaything of the leader, muddying the role of representatives in the law-making process. Politics and events decide which it is at any given moment.

Ways and means

As well as making laws, another major function of most legislatures is to monitor the tax and spend policies of the government. This began with the earliest assemblies, which were often established by monarchs seeking to raise money for specific purposes, known as 'ways and means'. But a report by the Association of Chartered Certified Accountants argued this was often more theoretical than real in

The filibuster

A symbol of the power of parliamentary procedure is the filibuster in the US Senate. Named after a Spanish word for piracy, it was designed to protect free speech by ensuring no time limit could be placed on debate. It has meant that legislation can be delayed or thwarted by senators talking for a long time. In some cases, a *very* long time. In June 1964 the southern Democrat Robert C Byrd spoke for 14 hours and 13 minutes to prevent the passage of the Civil Rights Act, which promised to outlaw racial discrimination. The law only passed because a large enough group of senators could be mustered to cut him off, using the procedure known as 'cloture'. The record for the longest filibuster is held by Strom Thurmond of South Carolina after he talked for more than 24 hours, which included reading from the phone book. James Stewart's use of the filibuster in the film *Mr Smith Goes to Washington* gave the process a romantic tinge but, for many, the real-life requirement to assemble 60 senators to silence one is a damaging brake on American democracy.

modern major democracies, such as the United Kingdom, Ireland, Australia and Canada. They worked on a system known as 'estimates' where members of parliament either approve or veto the entire annual programme of spending, with little genuine scrutiny of the details, or powers to amend lines in the budget.

An exception is the US Congress. It was given the power to 'to lay and collect Taxes, Duties, Imposts, and Excises' by the Constitution. Federal spending is only constitutional if it has been approved by Congress. This was a measure designed to limit the power of central government. But the inherent problems can be seen in the regular showdowns over the legal limit on the size of the US government's debt, the so-called 'debt ceiling'. These rows force the president to decide whether to spend money without authorization, to bust the debt rule or to raise taxes without permission – all illegal. Alternatively, the president might shut down the federal government, depriving more than three-quarters of a million workers of their paychecks and millions more of government services, or acquiesce to at least some of the budgetary demands of Congress.

How parliaments affect politics

'We shape our buildings and afterwards our buildings shape us,' said Winston Churchill as British members of parliament debated whether to replace the adversarial system of opposing green benches after bomb damage to the House of Commons in the Second World War. Churchill was speaking as much about rules of procedure as architecture because the institutional design of a legislature defines its power. Who sets the parliamentary agenda – the government or the institution itself? Can parliamentary committees compel witnesses to attend hearings so they can be held to account? Can members of an assembly veto an international treaty? How strong is party discipline? Do some actions require a super-majority of members, which means change on some issues might feel out of reach for a generation?

The condensed idea
Where the people are represented

25 Politicians

In his seminal lecture about professional politics in Munich, in 1919, the German sociologist Max Weber said that everyone was an 'occasional' politician, either because they voted in elections or they sought to influence political decisions in their favour. But then there were individuals for whom politics was a vocation, a calling. Weber divided them into two types – people who lived 'for' politics and people who lived 'off' politics. The first were those who liked having power or whose life was given meaning by being part of a cause. If a country was going to be run by this kind of person, then it would by necessity be dominated by people who were already independently wealthy. The second were those who became politicians to earn money. They would have to be paid a salary, or make money from 'tips and bribes' or receive some other advantage, Weber said.

Career politicians

The term 'career politician' was popularized by the British-Canadian Professor of Politics Anthony King in a 1981 article, 'The Rise of the Career Politician in Britain'. For King, 'career' was a more accurate word than 'professional', which applied to more formal occupations such as medicine, and a less loaded term than 'amateur'. It was still fairly loaded, though, with its connotation of sometimes trying to climb the greasy pole.

Mining diaries and autobiographies, King saw Weber's division between living 'for' or living 'off' politics in the reactions of two Conservative ministers as they left the British cabinet in the 1960s. One, Oliver Lyttelton, was a veteran of both of Winston Churchill's administrations. In his resignation letter, he wrote: 'I had a very disturbing conversation with my accountant who told me that I was rapidly exhausting my capital and that in fairness to my wife and children I should not continue in politics for any longer.' In contrast, Sir David Maxwell-Fyfe, who served three prime ministers over three decades, was distraught when his 'great political adventure' ended in his sacking. He confided in his memoirs: 'The great world of politics

> I have climbed to the top of the greasy pole.
> Benjamin Disraeli, 1868.

charmed me from the first time that I seriously beheld it. Over forty years later its fascination for me has not diminished . . . the world of politics entranced me.' The two Conservatives, both alike in role and background, left the scene with very different attitudes.

To provide empirical evidence for this theory of the rise of the career politician, King analysed the composition of the House of Commons from the 1930s to the 1970s. He found that members were increasingly being elected when they were in their 30s, suggesting they had not been working outside politics for long. They were retiring later, too, which led King to the conclusion that 'Old soldiers never die; old career politicians hang on for as long as they can.'

Female politicians

Female politicians outnumbered men in three parliaments at the start of 2023 – in Rwanda, Nicaragua and Cuba. There is a 50/50 gender split in a small handful of parliaments, but generally women are under-represented in politics in most countries.

The political scientists Sarah Anzia and Christopher Berry found that female politicians were more successful – if success was how much more funding a US congresswoman could obtain for their home district compared to a male representative. Electing a woman earned a constituency an extra $49 million a year on average, they calculated. The theory was that it was more difficult for women to get elected, so therefore only the toughest, most talented women would stand for office in the first place. And if electorates were sexist (as evidence suggested they were) and demanded higher standards from women than men, then only the very best female candidates would win. This has been referred to as the 'Jackie (And Jill) Robinson Effect' after Jackie Robinson became the first African American man to play Major League baseball in 1947. With so much racism at the time, he had to be better than any white baseball player to overcome the prejudice of club owners and fans.

The career politician was likely to be more thrusting and assertive. The consequences were that they would focus more on their constituents, seek alternative power bases, such as the chairmanship of parliamentary committees, and rebel more often against their party. These predictions have proved very prescient in British politics.

Where politicians come from

King also spotted that an increasing number of parliamentarians had worked in jobs such as teaching, lecturing, journalism and public relations. In other words, they were good communicators. And communicating had become the most important skill for the career politician. The number who had been lawyers remained consistently high, at around 14 per cent.

In 1858, an enormous 82 per cent of American Congressmen were lawyers and in 1883 President Woodrow Wilson wrote: 'The profession I chose was politics; the profession I entered was the law. I entered the one because I thought it would lead to the other.' Why was the number of lawyers-turned-politicians so high? For Max Weber, the law was the perfect training ground because it taught a person how to represent an interest (a client) and made them good with words. Others have theorized that nowadays it is because lawyers give political jobs to fellow lawyers, that law firms are more likely to grant time off for political campaigning or that wealthy lawyers donate campaign funds to other wealthy lawyers. According to one estimate, it means that an American lawyer is a hundred times more likely to be elected than an average citizen and ten times more likely to be elected than a millionaire.

But in the US Congress, lawyers are now outnumbered by people who have worked in public service or politics already. This trend of backroom operators running for office has also been seen in the United Kingdom, Australia, Canada and Germany, leading to concerns about the creation of a political culture that is removed from everyday life. Analysis of the Comparative Candidate Survey, which is completed by around 27,000 candidates in more than 20 countries, suggested that advisors-turned-elected representatives were likely to prioritize the needs of their political parties over their constituents. So many French politicians were graduates of one school, the École Nationale d'Administration (ENA) that there was a name for them –

énarques. Its closure was announced by the president as a concession to members of the *gilets jaunes* movement who were angry about elitism in French society.

The Parliament of Canada has the opposite phenomenon – the 'amateur politician'. Because elections are frequent and competition between political parties is fierce, members of parliament gain and lose office at quite a pace. This means there is a large turnover of politicians, and they tend to be politically inexperienced. The professional political classes have had less of a grip on the process for selecting candidates and so there are more teachers, farmers and businesspeople in parliament who then return to their schools, farms and companies after their time in politics.

The condensed idea
Politics is a profession

26 Leaders

'**T**o be prime minister of Canada you need the hide of a rhinoceros, the morals of St Francis, the patience of Job, the wisdom of Solomon, the strength of Hercules, the leadership of Napoleon, the magnetism of a Beatle, and the subtlety of Machiavelli.' Canadian Prime Minister Lester Pearson is reported to have given this formula for political leadership in the 1960s.

Biography or history?

What are the qualities that make a good political leader? Scholars of leadership have been split between the schools of Victorian writer Thomas Carlyle ('The history of the world is but the biography of great men') and Martin Luther King ('We are not makers of history. We are made by history'). In other words, between the character of individuals and the structures within which they operate and the events they face.

History has tended to trump biography, and academics will continue to argue about the right balance for ever. But the imagination of practising politicians has been captured by two texts about leadership. One is the much-misunderstood study of authority, *The Prince*, written in Renaissance Italy by Machiavelli. The other is the German father of sociology Max Weber's lecture to students in Munich, in 1919, the title of which has been translated into English as *Politics as a Vocation*.

The Prince

The former diplomat Niccolò Machiavelli wrote *The Prince* in around 1513 in the form of a letter to the ruler of Florence, Lorenzo de Medici, as a way to ingratiate himself. Much of the book was about how a prince could maintain control over conquered territory. This meant it often sounded brutal. Take Machiavelli's instruction about injuring someone: make it so serious that they are too weak to take revenge on you.

In Machiavelli's cynical view of human nature, people were a bundle of selfish emotions, which had consequences for a leader:

'From this arise the following question: whether it is better to be loved than feared, or the reverse. The answer is that one would like to be both the one and the other; but because it is difficult to combine them, it is far better to be feared than loved if you cannot be both.'

Being feared rather than loved was the better choice for a ruler because people's affections were fleeting, whereas fear was longer lasting. Less noticed has been Machiavelli's further warning that being hated or held in contempt were the worst outcomes.

From this flowed some rules for leadership. Be flexible. Ignore flattery. Delegate the unpopular decisions but own the good ones. Make sure punishments and rewards are high profile. Choose advisors carefully and never ask them a question that suggests weakness. Acknowledge that half of life is about 'fortune' (luck) not judgment. Combine the wiliness of a fox to avoid traps with the strength of a lion to get results. And do not worry too much about telling the truth.

This advice earned Machiavelli a historic reputation as the tyrant's friend. His advice applied in a pre-unification Italy that was riven by conflict, under constant attack from its neighbours and under the sway of the Church, but the leadership themes sketched out by Machiavelli have been seen in politics again and again and some sound totally modern. Take his warning that the prince who has spent too much 'will soon squander all his resources, only to be forced in the end, if he wants to maintain his reputation, to lay excessive burdens on the people.' In other words, unfunded public spending now means higher taxes in future – a soundbite from every election, ever.

Politics as a vocation

At the time of Max Weber's lecture in Munich, in January 1919, Germany was on the brink of a civil war and the Weimar Republic was still being established. The population was a mixture of the war-weary, the revolutionary young and soldiers who felt let down by their politicians. The title of the talk was *Politik als Beruf* – Politics as a Job. But the German word *Beruf* also means 'a vocation'; much more than a job. The audience was told that the character of politicians was of great importance because they controlled the state, which had in Weber's famous formulation 'the monopoly of the legitimate use of force.'

Wielding this power meant a good politician required three things: passion, a feeling of responsibility and a sense of proportion. This required him – and it was a 'him' throughout Weber's lecture – to balance the 'ethic of moral conviction' with the 'ethic of responsibility'. The first meant having a vision, and the second meant preserving the stability of society.

The biggest danger was the politician who used the coercive power of the state for their own 'quite vulgar vanity'; in the service of 'purely personal self-intoxication,' rather than for their goals. Good ends might require dubious means, and vice versa, Weber asserted. And the politician had to accept what this might do to him – 'He must know that he is responsible for what may become of himself under the impact of these paradoxes.'

Weber built towards a gloomy conclusion about the future of Germany, but ended with a rousing call, which also served as a warning to his countrymen:

'Politics is the long and slow boring of hard boards. It takes both passion and perspective. Certainly all historical experience confirms the truth – that man would not have attained the possible unless time and again he had reached out for the impossible, But to do that a man must be a leader, and not only a leader but a hero as well, in a very sober sense of the word ... Only he has the calling for politics who is sure that he shall not crumble when the world from his point of view is too stupid or too base for what he wants to offer. Only he who in the face of all of this can say "In spite of it all!" has the calling for politics.'

Earlier in the lecture, Weber complained that Germany's parliament was incapable of producing good leaders. Much better was the British House of Commons and its associated party machines, which toughened up their members. This created authoritative figures such as the Victorian Prime Minister William Gladstone, whom Weber christened 'the dictator of the battlefield of elections'. To Cambridge Professor David Runciman, the ideal politician in Weber's mould was the US President Abraham Lincoln – a trained lawyer (because law was good practice for politics), a party hack who lost frequently before he won, and who understood that thousands might die so that the United States could survive. The American public seems to agree. According to the polling company YouGov, Lincoln's popularity rating among Americans today is 79 per cent.

The executive

Regardless of their personal qualities, it is the political system that decides a leader's powers. In a republic, the head of state is usually a president. They can be a strong executive figure, such as the French president or, like the German president, they can be a symbolic figurehead for the whole nation and the country is really run by the chancellor. In the constitutional monarchy of the United Kingdom, the king is head of state and appoints the head of government, the prime minister, from within parliament. In the United States the roles of head of state and government are combined. But over recent decades each constitutional system has experienced the same phenomenon: an increased focus by voters and the media on the individuals vying for leadership, which scholars call 'personalization'. This suggests a return to fashion of Carlyle's 'great man' (for which, read 'person') theory of history.

The condensed idea
With great power comes great responsibility

27 Trade Unions

Historians have argued whether the guilds that represented craftsmen in the pre-industrial era were the basis for the modern-day trade union movement. What is clear, is that organizations that collectively represented the rights of tradesmen were fairly exclusive and focused on particular crafts. It was not until the economy became organized on a truly mass basis in the 19th century, however, that trade unions also became mass movements. This gave them power.

As a result, these organizations have often found themselves at the centre of big democratic moments. Trade unionists played a large role in the Chartist movement in the United Kingdom that fought successfully for the extension of the vote in the 19th century, and unions received official recognition under British law in 1867. American trade unionists forced an unwilling President Taft to create the Department of Labor in 1913 and then were instrumental in the fight for civil rights in the 1950s and 1960s. The Communist government in Poland was brought down in the 1980s by the shipyard union Solidarity. Nelson Mandela credited the Congress of South African Trade Unions (COSATU) with helping to end apartheid. Backed by their power to bring huge numbers of workers out on strike, unions delivered better pay, conditions, and innovations such as the 'weekend'.

But, according to the International Labour Organization (ILO), global trade union membership peaked in 1975 at around 35 per cent of the workforce and has been in decline ever since.

Declining union membership

Levels of union membership have roughly halved since the heyday of the 1970s, according to the ILO. But there are big variations from country to country. Iceland has the most unionized workforce, with a membership rate that has remained at around 91 per cent. In the middle of the pack were South Africa (29 per cent), Argentina (27 per cent) and the United Kingdom (23 per cent). Near the bottom of the table was the United States, where the level was 10 per cent of the workforce. At around 16 million American workers, this represents the lowest level on record.

The big theories for this change were a move from economies based on manufacturing (which tends to be highly unionized) to services (which tend to be less unionized) and, more recently, the increase in the so-called 'gig economy', in which workers occupy a grey zone between employment and freelancing.

But economists say this is not the whole story and point to many other factors that have contributed to the decline in union membership. There has been a rise in small firms, for example, and small firms are less likely to be unionized. Younger workers seem less likely to embrace union membership. And then there is the performance of the economy. Do workers leave unions and then return to them when high inflation means they want to fight for higher pay? Or is the defining factor government policies towards trade unions?

Governments v unions

The theme of the relationship between governments and unions since the late 1970s has primarily been one of the former cracking down on the latter.

In the United Kingdom, Margaret Thatcher's 1979 election landslide followed the 'Winter of Discontent' when a total of 29.5 million workdays were lost to strike action in a year and, infamously, the dead went unburied. Thatcher introduced reforms to end the so-called 'closed shop' – the rule that made union membership mandatory in some workplaces – and brought in higher thresholds for ballots for strike action.

The financial assistance received by southern European countries from international institutions during the Eurozone-crisis of 2010 came with strings attached. Often these required a reduction in union powers and collective bargaining rights. In Greece, trade unions led many of the protests against the bailouts that ended in violent clashes with the police.

Today it seems the strongest opposition to unions comes from large, well-known employers, such as tech companies and ride-sharing apps, which have found themselves battling workers, the courts and public opinion over the rights of their employees to organize. This has been accompanied by the rise of a new type of corporate job: the anti-union consultant.

Corporatism

The term 'corporatism' describes a situation where outside interests such as trade unions or business organizations have a formal role in the operation of the government. It comes from the Latin *corpus,* meaning 'body' or 'group' and was given a bad name by Mussolini's Fascist regime, which adopted corporatism as a way of running Italy in the 1920 and 1930s. Twenty-two corporations managed elements of national life, and members of the corporate bodies replaced the lower house of parliament. After the Second World War, political thinkers such as Philippe Schmitter tried to redeem the word to analyse relationships between governments and 'social partners'.

An example is the Dutch system for negotiating wages and hours known as the 'polder model'. It is named after the dykes that were constructed to prevent flooding in the low-lying country, and which became a symbol of co-operation between different communities. Corporatism has been criticized as undemocratic for undermining the role of elected parliamentarians and elevating vested interests. In the United Kingdom such arrangements were caricatured in the 1970s as union leaders being invited into government offices for 'beer and sandwiches' to jointly (mis) manage the economy.

Collective bargaining

But trade unions still possess a powerful tool to influence governments and employers – collective bargaining. This is when wage levels and employment conditions are negotiated for whole professions or economic sectors. When bargaining is nationwide and sectoral it is labelled as 'centralized'. When it happens at the level of individual firms, it is 'decentralized'. 'Organized decentralization' is when companies and workers strike their own deal but guided by national standards, with room for local trade-offs. If an agreement is *erga omnes* – the Latin phrase meaning 'towards everybody' – then it applies to all workers, not just union members. Labour organizations can co-operate. This happens annually with the Shunto or 'spring offensive' in Japan, for example, where hundreds of wage negotiations begin simultaneously in February.

Worldwide, a third of workers were covered by these collective deals in 2022, according to the ILO. Academics have identified a number of factors that contribute to the level of collective bargaining in a country: whether a country transitioned from communism to capitalism, whether it has a big public sector, which tends to mean a big union presence, and (again) if the government limited trade union power.

Workers' voices

Trade unions are not the only way workers can be represented in their workplaces. Others include workers' councils with defined powers, or via direct engagement in town hall meetings or internal referendums. All of these were bundled together in France in 2017 in a set of reforms known as the *ordonnances*. All large companies were obliged to set up powerful social and economic committees as a quid-pro-quo for making it easier to fire people, in a controversial attempt by President Emmanuel Macron to simplify France's 3,000-page labour code.

The economists Thomas Amossé and John Forth compared statistics between France, with its strong worker representation, and Britain where it is relatively weaker. The academics found that disgruntled French workers tended to launch (a lot of) industrial disputes, whereas unhappy British workers just quit instead.

In various ways, these alternative means of standing up to power – employee committees, trade unions, collective bargaining, worker-driven protest – have animated political movements from social democracy to anarchism and communism. Opposing them has been a major theme of politics in the last half century. For some politicians, such as Margaret Thatcher in the United Kingdom in the 1980s, the battle with trade unions defined them.

The condensed idea
Democracy at work

28 Influence

Bribery is illegal but happens. Lobbying is lawful but gives an advantage to those with access and resources. Influence is a necessary part of the democratic process but becomes illegitimate when it becomes 'undue'.

Corruption

The campaign group Transparency International ranks 180 countries in its annual Corruption Perceptions Index (CPI). A score of 0 is very corrupt; 100 is very 'clean'. In 2022, the average score was 43 out of 100, which has remained unchanged for a decade. Denmark, Finland and New Zealand were at the top. Somalia, Syria and South Sudan were at the bottom.

A 1,741-page account of how a government could be bribed was provided by the Charbonneau Commission, which investigated how contracts for public construction projects were awarded in the Canadian province of Quebec. Published in French in 2015, it looked at 15 years of transactions from 1996. An economist estimated this amounted to around a hundred million Canadian dollars' worth of business a year. The commission found that there had been collusion and corruption. The former saw companies agreeing deals between themselves, either to drop out of the bidding or to rotate their bids or to subcontract to each other when they won. The latter saw public officials receiving money, gifts or trips on a luxury yacht in return for contracts, and for more subtle acts such as tweaking selection criteria. Companies funded politicians, directly and indirectly. And then there was infiltration by organized crime, including the mafia and a motorbike gang. They provided loans, ran intimidation rackets and invested in projects via trade unions. Sixty recommendations were made, including stronger protections for whistle-blowers.

'Show me the money . . .'

Although outright bribery exists in most Western democracies, the anti-corruption expert Michael Johnson thought it was rare and described these countries as 'influence markets' instead. Using the examples of the United States, Germany and Japan he showed how money found its way through cracks inside and between democratic structures. In America, it was via political funding, where the incumbent candidate was almost always able to raise more money than a challenger, for example. In Japan it was a mixture of the '1941 system' where governments cooperated with industry and the '1955 system' which brought right-wing political parties together under one umbrella, a combination that led to some big commercial scandals.

Another concept is 'policy capture', which the wealthy countries' think-tank the Organisation for Economic Co-operation and Development (OECD) describes as 'the process of consistently or repeatedly directing public policy decisions away from the public interest towards the interests of a specific interest group or person.' Under the OECD definition, this could happen to entire governments ('state capture') or it could occur in the authorities that

Treating

William Hogarth's 1755 painting *Canvassing for Votes* hints at citizens being bribed for the support during a raucous election campaign in the fictional village of Guzzledown. In front of one of three inns pictured, the landlady of The Royal Oak is counting her earnings from hosting an election meeting. Fears that candidates were influencing voters with food and drink – and coal, in one case – led to the creation of the offence of 'treating' in British election law. The updated 1983 Representation of the People Act defined it as the offer of 'any meat, drink, entertainment or provision' for the purpose of 'corruptly influencing' a person. Both giver and the receiver can be found guilty.

A candidate in the United Kingdom's general election of 2015 avoided prosecution after they provided sausage rolls at an event. Police officers may have recalled a court judgment in a treating case from 1892, which said: 'It does not make it corrupt treating that a roof or warmth is provided for the meeting, nor is it necessarily corrupt treating if the persons attending the meeting are provided with some sort of refreshment. But if they are gathered together merely to gratify their appetites and so to influence their votes, then it is treating within the Act.'

Lobbying

Lobbying takes its name from the practice of grabbing legislators in the lobby to urge them to vote a certain way. The United States passed lobbying laws for the shipping and utilities industries in the 1930s. They passed a federal regulation in 1946 because Congress was dealing with so many big postwar issues that were ripe for influence-peddling, such as the electrification of rural areas and a big programme to build houses for war veterans. Its scope was limited by a judgment of the Supreme Court in 1954, and it was replaced in 1995. The American lobbying industry is known as 'K Street' because so many companies are located in that area of Washington, DC. The transparency campaigners OpenSecrets calculated that more than US$4 billion was spent on lobbying in the United States in 2022, with pharma companies spending the most. Brussels, the Belgian home of the EU's main institutions, hosts around 25,000 lobbyists.

Countries' lobbying laws have mainly focused on registers of practitioners and their activities, but some only cover third-party firms that are hired for this purpose and not in-house influencers. The implications of this in the United Kingdom became clear in 2021 when it emerged that the prime minister at the time of the British law's introduction, David Cameron, had lobbied ministers on behalf of a financial firm he joined after leaving office. Because he was an employee, he did not have to register as a lobbyist.

The United Kingdom and many other countries experience the phenomenon of 'the revolving door' where former ministers and officials leave office to work in the sectors they were recently overseeing. Some governments have introduced 'cooling off periods' ranging from three years in France to ... zero in Australia.

oversaw the economy ('regulatory capture'.) The causes of capture were a combination of the activities of politicians, public officials, intermediaries, brokers and lobbyists, which could be direct or indirect. The products could be systematic favouritism in public spending decisions, tax breaks or state-sponsored loans, or the granting of monopoly positions in supposedly competitive markets.

The OECD also highlighted two techniques that are used to shape opinions in a regulatory environment. One is 'astroturfing', where seemingly independent groups are funded by commercial interests. The other is 'smoke-screening', where vested interests fund research to cast doubt on negative evidence about their sector.

Influencers

And the concept of 'influencer' has existed far longer in politics than in social media. Think of the power of activists, celebrities, opposition political parties, charities, and think-thanks to sway the national conversation. The ancient Greeks even invented a group of intellectuals, the 'sophists', to steer public discussions. Getting the combination right leads to a vibrant, pluralistic society. In the 1950s, the theorist Robert Dahl tried to popularize the word 'polyarchy' – from the Greek words for 'many' and 'rule' – to describe a form of democracy where power lay in many hands. Get it wrong, and let influence accumulate in too few hands, then the result is an 'extractive' government that rules in the interests of the few and not the many. According to the title of the influential 2012 book by the academics Daron Acemoglu and James Robinson, this is the main reason 'why nations fail'.

The condensed idea
Everyone has influence but some can afford more

29 Church and State

At various points in history, the church *was* the state, or has been at war with the state, or has been curtailed by the state. The notion that they are separate things was discussed as early as the 5th century, when St Augustine contrasted The City of God with The City of Man following the conquest of Rome by pagans. Despite talking about states of mind rather than different types of government, St Augustine had made an early attempt to keep religion and politics apart.

Separation of church and state

The modern idea that government and religion should not mix is often credited to the authors of the US constitution. But the famous phrase 'the separation of church and state' never appears in the document. Instead, it comes from a ruling by the US Supreme Court in 1947 that allowed the state government of New Jersey to pay for parents to send their children to private religious schools by bus.

The justices ruled that this was just another public service, like roads. In their opinion, they wrote, the policy did not breach the 'wall between church and state' that Thomas Jefferson had referred to in a letter in 1802. Back then Jefferson was clarifying the First Amendment to the Constitution, which prevented the federal government interfering in the work of churches. This was designed to protect the freedom of religious expression, allowing religion to flourish while at the same time limiting the likelihood that one religion could dominate the life of the newly independent nation. (The idea was also central to the French Revolution, as a way of eliminating a source of authority that rivalled the power of the people.)

Secularism in theory

Policies that manage – some might say 'restrict' – the role of religion in national life are described as secularist. A useful contribution to this type of thinking was a lecture given in the Vatican in 2006 by the Archbishop of Canterbury at the time, Rowan Williams. The then leader of the world's 85 million Anglican Christians distinguished between two types of secularism.

The first was 'programmatic'. While accepting the liberal principles of respecting people's beliefs and butting out of their private lives on the one hand, this type of secularism excluded faith-based views from political debate on the other, fearing that religious dogma would dominate the public sphere. As a result, this approach 'finds specific views of the human good outside a minimal account of material security and relative social stability unsettling, and concludes that they need to be relegated to the purely private sphere,' the archbishop told his audience. He meant that liberal states were good at safeguarding personal freedoms but risked ignoring the common good and the need to address moral issues that transcended the lives of individuals. This focus on the autonomy of the individual could even become ruthless and descend into despotism (the tyranny of the individual rather than the majority). The answer, Williams argued in 2006, was 'procedural secularism', where faith was given a voice in important debates with moral dimensions: '. . . not necessarily one in which they are privileged or regarded as beyond criticism, but one in which they are attended to as representing the considered moral foundation of the choices and priorities of citizens.'

Secularism in action

In reality, countries that are formally secular can show a combination of both approaches set out by Rowan Williams. America's 'separation of church and state' means that daily prayers in school can be deemed unconstitutional, yet most children are expected to recite the pledge of allegiance every day ('I pledge allegiance to the flag of the United States of America, and to the republic for which it stands, one nation under God . . .'). Where the boundary lies between church and state has been tested in American courts again and again. In fact, some Supreme Court justices even disagreed with the judgment that gave the world the phrase in the first place, arguing that the New Jersey school bus policy was illegal because it favoured one religion over others.

And the implementation of secularism can be hotly contested. France has a policy of *laïcité* – respect for religious beliefs – but limits their expression and allows little or no role for them in decisions about how the country is run. It prevents the 'conspicuous' display of religious symbols. This makes it illegal to wear a full-face veil in public

Some countries are run entirely on religious principles. These are theocracies. The Oxford University constitutional expert Vernon Bogdanor defined them as places where 'God is recognized as the immediate ruler and His laws are taken as the legal code of the community and are expounded and administered by holy men as His agents.' Modern-day theocracies include the Vatican, Saudi Arabia and Iran.

The Iranian revolution of 1978–9 swept the authoritarian shah from power and ushered in a new regime under Ayatollah Khomeini. The new constitution had Islamic law at its heart and made a *faqih* – a senior theologian – the head of state. The role of Islam in the state was further entrenched. A new penal code introduced corporal punishment such as hanging for crimes from adultery to blasphemy. The families of victims of crimes were given the right to seek retribution against the perpetrators. Constitutional amendments abolished the office of prime minister and gave new powers to the directly elected president but most of all strengthened the role of the supreme leader. In the words of the Harvard academic H E Chehabi, it meant that 'instead of a society governed by Islamic law, citizens were given the duty to obey an absolute ruler.'

The leader is chosen by the Assembly of Experts, made up of Islamic scholars. The president appoints ministers, who are approved by the elected parliament, the Majles. A 12-member Council of Guardians – half Islamic jurists, half civil law experts – decides whether legislation is compatible with the constitution and Islamic law.

Campaigners for a more moderate Iranian regime, both inside and outside the country, have experienced optimism and disappointment in equal measure, from seemingly reform-minded presidents who were unable to reform very much to grassroots protests led by female students that promised change but were then violently suppressed.

places, for example. The tougher application of this principle after Islamist terrorist attacks has led to the French government being accused of Islamophobia.

The feeling that secularism can be a form of discrimination against Muslims has been harnessed by the Turkish president Recep Tayyip Erdogan. He has challenged the religious neutrality that has been a cornerstone of modern Turkey. Historically, state employees have been prevented from wearing headscarves. The government has regulated religious institutions. Turkish ID cards state the holder's faith. To believers in secularism this has guaranteed equality. To many Turkish Muslims it has felt like a lack of respect or discrimination, and appealing to them has helped a progressively less secular-sounding Erdogan to win three presidential elections.

The United Kingdom fudges formal and informal approaches to the mixture of politics and religion by having Christian bishops in the upper chamber of Parliament, a head of state (the monarch) who is also the head of the Church of England and, in 2022, its first Hindu prime minister whose faith is rarely remarked upon.

The condensed idea
Balancing god and politics

30 Monarchy

The basis of republicanism is the rejection of monarchy. Thomas Paine demolished the concept of royalty and inspired the American colonists to seek independence from the British king, George III, in his essay of 1776, *Common Sense*. To the passionate pamphleteer, the 'exceedingly ridiculous' institution was sinful, corrupt and failed to fulfil the advantages attributed to it, such as preventing civil wars. Historically, Paine argued, monarchs had been appointed in ways that lacked legitimacy: by lot (random), by election (like a politician) or by usurpation (violence).

The hereditary principle, where crowns are handed down from parent to child, made monarchy even worse in Paine's eyes, leading

A thirst for absolute power is the natural disease of monarchy.
Thomas Paine

him to conclude: 'In short, monarchy and succession have laid . . . the world in blood and ashes. Tis a form of government which the word of God bears testimony against, and blood will attend it.' (Although the members of the original American republican movement that he inspired have been criticized for being elitist landowners whose domination of women and slaves was little better than the oppressive rule by the British king.)

The English constitution

A century later, British journalist Walter Bagehot made the opposite case to Paine's in *The English Constitution* (1873). He argued that the British system received five benefits from its monarch, then Queen Victoria.

Firstly, the governance of a country with one person at its head was easier to grasp than a republic, where power was diffused. 'The mass of mankind understand it, and they hardly anywhere else in the world understand any other,' he wrote. Secondly, it incorporated religion, which meant the head of state was viewed with 'mystic awe and wonder'. Thirdly, the queen was head of 'society' – wealthy, cultured families – which provided a contrast with the political class, who Bagehot described as 'social adventurers'. Fourthly, the behaviour of the monarch imported an element of morality into the system. Finally, the queen provided a disguise to 'enable our real rulers to change, without heedless people knowing it.'

Some of Bagehot's analysis of regal power has gone out of date. For example, he wrote about the British monarch's authority to appoint the prime minister. Nowadays that right is more symbolic than real. Similarly, their previous ability to dissolve parliament and call an election is now firmly in the hands of the PM. New members of the second chamber, the House of Lords, are chosen by the political parties and merely approved – not decided – by the monarch. New legislation receives 'royal assent' as its final stage before becoming law – but with a metaphorical rubber stamp rather a power of veto.

A few of Bagehot's instructions have earned the status of timeless royal textbook. He said the monarch had the right to 'consult, encourage and warn' the government of the day. This formed the basis of the relationship between Queen Elizabeth II and her 15 prime ministers, from Winston Churchill in 1952 to short-lived Liz Truss in 2022. Bagehot also advised that 'We must not let daylight upon magic,' which has informed the House of Windsor's policy of 'never explain, never complain' in the face if negative news coverage.

The Crown in Parliament

According to Walter Bagehot, the long historic tussle between Crown and Parliament has meant that, in the United Kingdom, 'A Republic has insinuated itself beneath the folds of a Monarchy'. This set-up is often described as a constitutional monarchy. In practical terms it means that there is *a* sovereign (the king) but Parliament *is* sovereign. This creates some anomalies, such as the speech read out by the monarch at the opening of each new session of parliament, which sets out the priorities of 'my government' but that is written for them by the government. To fund his duties, the monarch receives public money known as the Sovereign Grant. This is calculated as 15 per cent of the annual profits from the royal family's holdings of public land. In 2022/23 this was £86.3 million. The House of Windsor also possesses great private wealth.

According to the British Social Attitudes survey, an authoritative source of public opinion that stretches back four decades, support for the institution spiked among British citizens in 2022 around Queen Elizabeth II's Platinum Jubilee and her death. But the number of citizens saying that the monarchy is 'very important' then dropped to its lowest level since researchers started collecting the data in 1983.

Modern republicanism

The overthrow of the Shah of Iran marked the victory of the Islamic Revolution in 1979. The election of Maoists to government in Nepal in 2008 led to the abolition of the country's 240-year-old Hindu monarchy. The institution had been damaged in 2001 when the crown prince killed the king and seven others in a palace massacre. Most modern republicanism is found in Britain's former colonies, 14 of which are 'realms' of the British monarch.

Barbados became a full republic in November 2021, following a unanimous vote in its parliament. There was no referendum, but it was the culmination of a movement to remove the monarch that began when the Caribbean country declared constitutional independence from the United Kingdom in 1966. The two nations bent over backwards to indicate there were no hard feelings at the handover ceremony, which was attended by the Prince of Wales and the singer Rihanna.

The last ex-British colony to do this had been Mauritius in 1992. Both nations remained members of the Commonwealth, the loose association of former British possessions. Polling by the Conservative Party donor Lord Ashcroft, on the eve of the coronation of Charles III in 2023, showed that a majority of the public wanted to remove the king as head of state in six Commonwealth countries: Antigua and Barbuda (47 per cent), Australia (42 per cent), the Bahamas (51 per cent), Canada (47 per cent), the Solomon Islands (59 per cent) and Jamaica (49 per cent). The last has established a constitutional commission to plan the transition to a republic. The Australian public voted for the status quo in 1999 and has made smaller steps to assert its independence since, such as designing new bank notes without the image of the monarch.

Among political philosophers, such as Philip Pettit of Princeton University, republicanism is deeper than opposition to a king or queen. It refers to the removal of all forms of command over individuals. This harks back to the Roman Republic, which was designed around laws and institutions that prevented domination of individuals by others (dominium) and of citizens by the state (imperium). This type of republican would argue that even a benevolent leader who promises to leave you alone is exerting control by making out that this is a favour.

The condensed idea
The King and Us

31 The Fourth Estate

I n pre-revolutionary France, three estates made up society: the clergy, the aristocracy and then everyone else, from peasants to the bourgeoisie. In the 19th century, a fourth was added: the media. The phrase 'fourth estate' was the invention of English essayist William Hazlitt, who used it in 1821 to describe the influence on public life of the farmer, radical journalist and polemicist, William Cobbett.

Hazlitt said of Cobbett: 'His style stuns his readers . . . he is too much for any single newspaper antagonist, "lays waste" a city orator or Member of Parliament, and bears hard upon the government itself. He is a kind of Fourth Estate in the politics of this country.' Cobbett's weekly *Political Register* was one of 477 papers established in England in the first half of the 19th century. A new way of holding power to account, many were deeply partisan, hyper local, personality led and held scant regard for the truth. Sound familiar?

Leap forward a few centuries to Barack Obama and his pre-presidential memoir, *The Audacity of Hope*, in which he suggests that people rely on the news in order to engage with democracy. He says: 'I – like every politician at the federal level – am almost entirely dependent on the media to reach my constituents . . . I am who the media says I am.'

A feral beast?

Obama was just about to find out what life was like as a leader in a world of 24/7 news. Someone who already knew was the outgoing British prime minister, Tony Blair. In 2007 he dedicated one of several farewell speeches to the state of journalism. After a decade in office, Blair sounded exhausted: 'I am going to say something that few people in public life will say, but most know is absolutely true: a vast aspect of our jobs today – outside of the really major decisions, as big as anything else – is coping with the media, its sheer scale, weight and constant hyperactivity. At points, it literally overwhelms.'

Blair acknowledged his own party's reputation for using the media to get elected – 'It was hard to see any alternative' – but savaged the way reporters had come to cover politics. He said there were five consequences. Scandal had become more important than straight news. Questioning the motives of ministers was more exciting than assessing their judgment. Interpreting the behaviour of politicians and commentary on politics was replacing reporting. Opinions, which were valid on their own and labelled as such, were becoming mixed with fact. And the fear of missing out on a story meant that correspondents hunted as a pack 'just tearing people and reputations to bits'. He then infamously described the media as a 'feral beast', which gave everyone their headline for the day.

Trends

Blair's speech was given in another era. Some of the trends he mentioned have continued, such as the decline in audiences for daily TV news programmes and the circulation figures of printed newspapers. He was also correct about the growth in opinion-based media. Since Blair left office, the United Kingdom has since imported from the United States the idea of the TV and radio host with views, based on a novel interpretation of the long-standing British rule that broadcasters should be impartial. (The talk radio station LBC balances its presenters' views across the day, rather than insisting they never share their opinions, for example.) Elsewhere this manifested in hyper-partisanship or state-controlled media. In 2023, for example, a documentary showed the Indian news anchor Ravish Kumar answering his phone to death threats and having to flee cafes because his criticism of the government stood out in a news media that was becoming increasingly supportive of Prime Minister Narendra Modi.

News websites existed when Blair left office but one medium was in its infancy – social media. Facebook had only become available to the general public a year before Blair gave the 2007 speech. The Reuters Digital News Report of June 2023 provided a comprehensive take on how people get their news online, based on surveys of 94,000 people in 46 markets. It contained several shocks for journalists working for traditional outlets. Although there were geographical variations, fewer users were accessing the news via the apps and websites of legacy

Does the media lead or follow?

Political scientists have struggled to prove whether the media creates public opinion or follows it. Research around British general elections suggests that voters make up their own minds, but newspapers can influence the issues used in reaching a decision. Politicians have tended to follow their own self interest, cosying up to friendly outlets (Donald Trump and Fox News) and bashing them when they think it loses them votes (Donald Trump and CNN). Trump proved that politicians could swerve mainstream media and use social media to talk directly to voters, but few others have the same reach and still have their message mediated by the media.

media brands. Instead they were coming via the 'side doors' of social media, search engines and news aggregators, giving those companies enormous influence. The 'duopoly' of Google and Facebook's parent company Meta was losing some of its power as a gatekeeper to upstarts such as TikTok, but this meant even more platforms for journalists to feed in order to stay relevant. Consumers trusted algorithms to choose their news to the same extent they trusted professional editors. Younger users preferred getting their information from celebrities and influencers rather than journalists. And 36 per cent of people said they avoided the news, either partly or altogether.

It can sometimes feel like a return to William Cobbett's time – a confusing cacophony of outlets and opinions, and a voice for everyone. It brings to mind another speech by another figure who has been credited with popularizing the phrase 'the fourth estate', the Scottish philosopher Thomas Carlyle. In an 1840 lecture at Cambridge University about the power of the written word, he said:

> 'Whoever can speak, speaking now to the whole nation, becomes a power, a branch of government, with inalienable weight in law-making, in all acts of authority. It matters not what rank he has, what revenues or garnitures, the requisite thing is, that he have a tongue which others will listen to.'

In other words, it is not just professional journalists who hold a place in the fourth estate – it is now anyone who can command attention.

The condensed idea
Mediators of democracy

32 Courts

The rule of law is an essential element in the bundle of concepts that make a democracy. So, democracy needs courts. Some courts have been given political tasks as part of their official remit, whereas others have had politics thrust upon them by the changing nature of modern government and international affairs.

Constitutional courts

Some countries have specific courts with mandates to decide whether decisions made by the legislature or government comply with the constitution. Conceived by the Austrian legal expert Hans Kelsen, these so-called 'constitutional' courts were originally introduced in western Europe after the Second World War but are now found in

The US Supreme Court

'The Judicial power of the United States shall be vested in one Supreme Court,' says Article III, Section 1 of the US Constitution. It created arguably the most powerful branch of the US federal government. The nine justices of the Supreme Court decide how a document written more than two centuries ago is applied in the modern world, with consequences for the whole country. Judges represent particular interpretations of the Constitution, so the court's composition matters. Justices serve for life, giving the president immense power when making an appointment.

Some judgments have been epoch-defining. For example, in Brown v Board of Education of Topeka (1954), the court ruled that separate schools for white and Black children were unconstitutional, creating a legal basis for the civil rights movement. In Roe v Wade (1973) the court placed constraints on states' ability to limit access to abortion, based on a woman's right to privacy under the constitution. Further cases added and took away abortion rights.

almost a hundred countries, from France to Colombia to Taiwan. Some of them have the power to rule on laws before they are passed by the legislature, others only after a law has become *the* law. Some allow referrals only from other courts, some from politicians, a few from private citizens.

One of the most powerful is Germany's Federal Constitutional Court, opened in 1951. From their benches in the city of Karlsruhe, judges have ruled on the rights of political parties to exist, on whether East and West Germany could be reunified, and even on whether the German government had to comply with the ransom demands of a terrorist group that had kidnapped an industrialist (it did not).

These types of court are found in 'centralized' systems. 'Decentralized' systems allow other courts to rule on constitutional matters, with an 'apex' court making the most momentous decisions. The parliamentary systems in Canada, the United Kingdom and New Zealand place limits on the power of the courts because it is parliament that is supposed to possess sovereign power to define the (unwritten) constitution.

Courts ruling on politics

The intervention by judges in the 2000 US presidential election between George W Bush and Al Gore might seem like a rare foray by judges into questions of political leadership but it was not unusual. In 2009 Fiji endured a political crisis when its constitutional court ruled that a 2006 military coup was illegal, making the interim government unlawful, too. The prime minister stood down and the president took over. The president then fired the judiciary, reinstated the prime minister and introduced a new constitution several years later.

The South Korean Supreme Court ended the premiership of the country's first democratically elected prime minister Park Geun-hye in 2017 when it upheld parliament's decision to impeach her over allegations of corruption. A few years earlier the court had reversed the impeachment of another prime minister, Roh Moo-hyun.

Reform of the judicial system can land leaders in serious political trouble. In 2023 Israeli prime minister Benjamin Netanyahu paused changes to the court system in the face of the country's largest ever protests. Important elements of the conflict between Brussels and the governments of Hungary and Poland have been changes to the retirement age for judges and appointments to the bodies that oversee their work.

Judicial review

The general term for the ability of courts to scrutinize the actions of the state is 'judicial review'. In the United Kingdom it is limited to questioning the lawfulness of decisions made by public bodies rather than the right- or wrongness of a decision. The use of judicial review became a major political issue after two significant rulings by the UK Supreme Court. The first, in 2017, was over who had the right to trigger the process of leaving the EU: the government or Parliament? The government lost. The second, in 2019, was whether the prime minister could prorogue – suspend – Parliament during negotiations with the EU. The government lost again. Ministers commissioned a panel of experts to examine the system for signs that judicial review was being abused.

Despite the headline-grabbing examples, the study found that the number of judicial reviews had been falling (apart from the number of challenges to immigration decisions, which had exploded by as much as 30 per cent in some years). The other policy areas most likely to be subject to judicial review related to prisons, town planning and housing. The UK study is useful because it shows the types of decision that are sent to court for judicial review in a modern democracy.

And many of those immigration cases concerned human rights. Legal scholars say that the growth of human rights laws – both at a national level and an international level with the European Convention on Human Rights – has shifted a large subset of decisions about people's lives from politicians to judges.

International courts

The growth of international justice since the Second World War has seen transnational courts playing a bigger role in domestic politics. Benedict Kingsbury of New York University identified at least ten different types of international judicial body.

A prominent example is the European Court of Human Rights (ECHR) in the French city of Strasbourg, which considers cases from 46 of the countries that have signed the European Convention on Human Rights. (Russia was expelled after the invasion of Ukraine.)

In 2022 the ECHR examined 39,570 cases. Decisions were delivered in around 10 per cent of them, with the vast majority thrown out or deemed inadmissible. The countries subject to the most complaints were Turkey, Russia and Ukraine. Notable judgments that year included euthanasia laws in Belgium, how far Greek coastguards should go to rescue migrants at sea, whether France had a duty to re-admit a woman who had joined the civil war in Syria or whether the UK government could relocate a migrant to Rwanda. The political sensitivity of these subjects has often seen the judges accused of 'judicial activism' or 'over-reach' by domestic politicians who felt thwarted by them. (The ECHR should not be confused with the European Court of Justice, which interprets European Union law.)

A complaint made by many campaigners is that a secret network of international courts free of public scrutiny has been created by the growth of free trade agreements. This is because many deals include mechanisms whereby conflicts between companies and governments are settled behind closed doors in tribunals, rather than in national or international courts. These Investor State Dispute Settlement (ISDS) clauses became controversial in the 2010s after a series of high-profile trade negotiations. Stung by the criticism that issues important to farmers, businesses and consumers were escaping democratic oversight, the EU has moved away from ISDS clauses in recent trade talks.

'In sum, over the last few decades the world has witnessed a profound transfer of power from representatives to judiciaries, whether domestic or supranational,' concluded the Israeli legal and political scholar Ran Hirschl. He invented a new word to convey the growing power of judges over politicians – 'juristocracy'.

The condensed idea
Politicians decide, judges rule

33 Money

Politics and elections do not come cheap. Political parties spent an estimated US$8.6 billion on the 2019 national and state elections in India, for example. There are strong feelings about where politicians get their money from and what they spend it on. Heads of government have left office over party funding scandals, and many voters would agree with the American journalist Theodore H White, who wrote in 1984 that 'The flood of money that rushes into politics today is a pollution of democracy.'

The United States

In the US presidential election of 2020, Donald Trump spent US$744 million over two years, according to the database of the Federal Election Commission. In the same period, Joe Biden's campaign spent just over US$1 billion. The wealthy businessman Michael Bloomberg shelled out a similar amount on his independent run for president before he dropped out of the race and supported Biden. American political donations are split into four categories: individuals who give less than $200, individuals who give a lot more (such as the financier George Soros who donated US$170m during the midterms in 2022), committees formed to support political causes, or funds from the candidates themselves (such as Bloomberg's mostly self-funded campaign.)

The American system distinguishes between financial contributions to politics that are 'soft' and 'hard'. The former is spent on more general 'party-building' purposes or on issues such as healthcare or gun control. The latter is direct spending on candidates. Campaigners for reform of the political funding system refer to a third type: 'dark' money. By this they mean funds where the identity of the donor is not clear due to a lack of transparency in how donations are recorded.

The biggest change to the ways in which American politics is funded came in 2010 after two rulings by the US Supreme Court. These created so-called 'super-PACs', where PAC stands for political action committee. The forerunners to these committees were formed after the Second World War so that companies, trade unions and other organizations could bundle together donations to spend them on candidates or causes.

In Citizens United v Federal Election Commission, a right-wing campaign group fought for the right to air a TV documentary criticizing Hillary Clinton close to polling day in the 2016 presidential election. In their finding, a majority of justices agreed that the Constitution justified the broadcast of the programme because 'All speakers, including individuals and the media, use money amassed from the economic marketplace to fund their speech, and the First Amendment protects the resulting speech.' This and a later case, SpeechNOW.org v Federal Election Commission, established that it would be illegal for the government to place a limit on the amount that third parties such as businesses and unions could spend on political activities. This allowed the creation of committees that could spend unlimited sums, as long as they were not promoting a specific candidate or acting on their instructions. Collectively super-PACS spent around US$1 billion during the 2020 election, roughly the same amount as Joe Biden's campaign and more than Donald Trump's.

Spending limits

The other side of the coin is how much politicians are allowed to spend when they are campaigning. Roughly half of countries have limits. In the United Kingdom, the caps for candidates kick in during a defined period before polling day. They are entitled to spend £8,700 plus 6p per voter in mostly urban seats or 9p per voter in mostly rural seats. And they must report to the watchdog – the Electoral Commission – the cost of their advertising, staff, travel and leaflets. British political parties can spend what they like on party activities, with limits in the year before an election. Sometimes opponents challenge whether spending has benefitted the party or the individual. In the United States, there are limits on the spending by presidential candidates but only if they receive public funding.

Super-PACS either 'level the playing field' and empower grassroots campaigners, according to the Republican Senator Ted Cruz, or are a form of 'legalized bribery' in the words of the Democratic Senator Bernie Sanders.

Public funding

Public funding of political parties by the tax payer has often been presented as a solution to the problem of politicians having to solicit donations, and the fear of corruption that comes with it. Various versions of this exist. Canada bans companies and trade unions from donating to parties but offers subsidies for donations by individuals in the form of tax credits of up to 75 per cent, and allows candidates to claim up to 60 per cent of their election expenses. German political parties receive, on average, a third of their income from the government, often exceeding the contributions they get from their members. This has not made Germany immune to political funding scandals, however, such as one that engulfed the Christian Democrats in the early 1990s, which involved secret bank accounts and suitcases filled with cash. It led to the downfall of Chancellor Helmut Kohl and the rise of Angela Merkel. In Ireland, the receipt of public money is linked to parties reaching a threshold of 40 per cent female candidates. Sweden's Social Democrats have raised thousands by selling lottery tickets and scratch cards, a fund-raising tool that has been questioned on moral grounds.

In the United Kingdom, opposition parties receive so-called Short money from the House of Commons to help them hold the government to account. It is named after the Labour Party politician Edward Short, who told the House of Commons in 1974: 'The health of a democracy necessarily reflects the standing and independence of its political parties. For this reason, many Western democratic countries think it best that their political parties should have part of their finance provided from public funds.' For the modern Labour Party, this amounted to £6.5 million in 2021. The United Kingdom has tended to review its system of political funding at least once a decade but there has been little appetite to ask the public to pay for their politicians or to restrict political donations, either from the individuals and businesses that are relied upon by the Conservative Party or from the trade unions that fund Labour.

Digital adverts

But the latest review of the system in the United Kingdom, conducted by the Committee on Standards in Public Life in 2021, found there was 'an urgent need' to regulate a new type of political spending: adverts on the internet and social media. In a country where election campaigns mainly used to be fought with billboards on the street, 54 per cent of the spending on advertising in the British general election of 2019 was on Facebook, Twitter, Google and Snapchat. Who funded these adverts was not always clear, the committee concluded. Another recent threat has been the influence of foreign money. Many countries have banned donations from abroad, with most Western democracies fearing influence by Russia and, increasingly, China.

The condensed idea
Politics is not free

34 Constitutions

'**W**e the People of the United States, in Order to form a more perfect Union, establish Justice, insure domestic Tranquility, provide for the common defense, promote the general Welfare, and secure the Blessings of Liberty to ourselves and our Posterity, do ordain and establish this Constitution for the United States of America.'

The National Archives in Washington, DC, is like a shrine to the Constitution, a document with semi-sacred status in the United States. In a room kept deliberately dark to prevent fading, the four large pieces of parchment are displayed under glass in a case pumped full of preserving argon gas.

Some of the American colonies had adopted written constitutions before the framers met in Philadelphia in 1789 to draft a model for a federal United States. And texts setting out rules for the ruling and the ruled existed long before, such as the stone slabs of instructions from ancient Mesopotamia that have been discovered in the Middle East or Magna Carta, which was agreed between the English king and the wealthy barons at Runnymede in 1212. But the American Constitution and the documents produced during the French Revolution at around the same time encouraged the boom in written constitutions that began in the middle of the 18th century.

The contents of constitutions

The Constitution Unit at University College London counts around 200 written constitutions around the world. They all have in common the idea that some of the ways in which a political system operates should be written down. They are 'concerned with the grandest and most important of issues – the relationship between the individual and the state, the conditions of political order, and the methods by which men and women are ruled,' wrote British constitutional expert and Oxford University tutor to future prime ministers Professor Vernon Bogdanor.

But constitutions vary in length. At more than 145,000 words and 395 articles, India's is the longest. Around two-thirds of it is based on pre-independence legislation passed by the British House of

Commons when India was a colony, serving as a reminder that these documents can have as much backstory as any novel. Compare this with Monaco's version, which is only 3,814 words.

They also vary in the level of detail they provide, from the bold to basics. Article 9 of the Japanese constitution makes war illegal. Article 99 of Belgium's sets the number of ministers in the cabinet and how many must speak French or Dutch, to represent the country's two main communities. The US Constitution is made up of seven articles and many staples of American life are not in them, for example the right to privacy or the right to remain silent on arrest.

A new history of constitutions

The authors of constitutions also have varied reasons for writing them. This becomes clear in the 2021 revisionist history *The Gun, the Ship and the Pen*, by the Princeton historian Linda Colley. The title reflects her argument that constitutions were less a result of noble endeavours, more a product of wars and revolutions. Colley links episodes of growth in the number of written constitutions around the world to major outbreaks of violence – the American and French Revolutions, the end of the First and Second World Wars, the collapse of the Soviet Union after the Cold War, and a series of civil wars in the 1990s.

She argues that the documents served different purposes in different places. Some were created as bargains between governments and citizens to justify conscription in an era of mass warfare. They were sometimes written to consolidate new countries that emerged from the disintegration of empires (Austria), or as an act of strength by weaker countries in the face of domineering neighbours (Ireland). They could be used to make grand political statements, such as the need to emancipate labour and reduce inequality (Mexico and the Soviet Union), or to impose coherence on diverse territories (China).

She also points to the importance of cheap printing, which gives constitutions a mass readership and symbolic value, concluding her book with a picture of a protestor in South Africa who went viral after he hid his face with a pocket-sized copy of the text agreed by Nelson Mandela following the end of apartheid. Hailing from Britain where there is no written constitution, Colley presents herself as a 'candid friend' of these documents and warns they need constant attention if they are to work well.

Britain's unwritten constitution

The United Kingdom does not have a written constitution. Or does it? As if inventing *The Economist* newspaper was not enough of an achievement, in 1867 the genius political journalist Walter Bagehot also immortalized the idea that Britain had an 'unwritten' constitution. In his seminal work *The English Constitution* he analysed the relationships between Britain's institutions – parliament, government and monarchy. These amounted to a constitution that was made up of two parts. The first, which he called 'dignified', was 'one to excite and preserve the reverence of the population' and included the royal family. He named the second half 'efficient' because it concerned the 'work of government'.

A few decades later, A V Dicey wrote in his introduction to the *Study of Law of the Constitution* (1885) that Britain could never have a written constitution because this would trample over the most important aspect of the sovereignty of the British parliament – that no parliament could bind its successor. A written set of rules would constrain future parliamentarians. But centuries later the constitutional expert Vernon Bogdanor wrote: 'We are now in transition from a system based on parliamentary sovereignty to one based on the sovereignty of a constitution, albeit a constitution that is inchoate, indistinct and still in large part uncodified. But we are gradually becoming a constitutional state.' He cited Britain's then-membership of the European Union (which came with European treaties that looked quite like written constitutions), the 1998 Human Rights Act (which guaranteed certain rights in written form) and laws that made the United Kingdom more reminiscent of a federation (separate governments for Scotland, Wales and Northern Ireland and directly elected mayors for English cities).

How are they interpreted?

'The genius of the constitution rests not in any static meaning it might have had in a world that is dead and gone, but in the adaptability of its great principles to cope with current problems and needs,' William Joseph Brennan told students at Georgetown University in 1985. As an associate justice of the US Supreme Court, he was one of only nine people alive at any one time who have the life-long power to interpret the Constitution at a nationwide level.

The interpretation of written constitutions is split into two broad schools. The first includes those who believe the documents are 'living' and are comfortable applying old constitutional principles in new ways to handle modern problems. They cite the broad language used in the texts – the prohibition of 'cruel and unusual punishment' or that 'all people are equal before the law', for example – as evidence that they are supposed to be flexible.

Originalists, on the other hand, believe the power of a constitution rests in the intentions of the original authors, and are timeless. This does not mean a very strict interpretation is inevitable because some originalists are prepared to be creative. And their response to the argument that they are living in the past would be: 'OK, then amend the constitution for the present.'

Constitutions frequently contain clauses for their own amendment, usually with high thresholds for doing so, such as super-majorities in parliament or of the public. While some have hardly changed at all in over 50 years and have come to resemble ancient Mesopotamian stone tablets, Ireland has adapted its constitution more than 30 times since the 1970s.

The condensed idea
The power of the written word

35 The Ballot

I n his short story, *The Watcher*, Cuban-born author Italo Calvino describes a day in the life of a young man assigned to watch a general election unfold in Naples, in 1953. He is posted at a polling station in an institution for mentally ill and disabled people run by the Church. The corruption and confusion the watcher sees as nuns help voters make their decisions are used by Calvino as a metaphor for the democratic process as a whole – just as dropping a slip of paper into a box (or increasingly, tapping a box on a screen) has become *the* defining symbol of democracy.

Voting today

According to the ACE Knowledge Network, established in 1998 by the United Nations to collect data about the administration and costs of elections, 91 per cent of the countries that hold elections use paper ballots that voters mark with either a cross or numbers.

The network's data shows that electronic devices are used in 22 countries, including the United States, where there are geographical variations because the responsibility for organizing elections lies with individual states and not the federal government, even in the vote for president. Around a third of Americans vote via machine, usually a touchscreen. The majority use paper ballots that are then counted electronically. These methods were the basis for Donald Trump's disputed claims of fraudulent voting in 2020, and the source of an expensive legal dispute between the Fox News channel and the makers of the machines.

Some states used to use machines with which voters punched a hole in a card to indicate their preference. There was a drop-off in their use after some badly punched cards in Florida led to the 2000 election between George W Bush and Al Gore being settled in the Supreme Court. Another retro-sounding method has survived, though. Americans can still vote by fax, although in doing so they have to give up their right to a secret ballot and accept that a faulty transmission might mean they are denied a vote.

Modern technology is gradually creeping into voting processes across the world. In Oman, municipal councils were elected via a mobile phone app named Intakhib in December 2022 – a small concession to the protestors of the Arab Spring who demanded much larger constitutional reforms to the monarchy. Estonians have been able to vote online since 2005, thanks to the introduction of digital identity cards and society's embrace of web-based public services. The parliamentary elections of 2023 were the first in the Baltic state in which a majority chose to vote in this way. The delivery of hard drives to the counting centre is a big moment on Estonian election night. Citizens can change their minds until the close of polling to reduce the risk of being coerced to vote a certain way. But the system has been criticized as unsafe by some Estonian politicians, cybersecurity experts and international election observers.

These methods might be news to voters in the United Kingdom, where a regular feature of elections has been the question of whether ballot papers should be marked in pencil or ink. There is no legal requirement for either, but officials recommend the use of pencils to stop ink blots spoiling the vote. This has encouraged a persistent conspiracy theory that the state mandates pencil so that votes can be changed later.

Secret votes

It seems sacred that voting is secret. The anonymous ballot was introduced by the Romans in a series of reforms to electoral law in the second half of the second century BC. Historians have been divided on whether secret ballots were a move by the wealthy to hold on to power or to share it with the people; whether it eliminated bribery or provided more opportunities for it. Cicero captured some of the contemporary debate about it, when one of his characters Quintus explained to another how it was a bad idea from the point of view of the elites (known as the 'optimates' and the 'boni'):

'Everyone knows that the ballot law has deprived the optimates of all their influence . . . The people should not have been provided with a hiding place, where they could conceal a mischievous vote by means of the ballot, and keep the boni in ignorance of their real opinions. For these reasons no good citizen has ever proposed or supported a measure like yours.'

Like the principles of, and arguments about, democracy, the oldest elements of voting are found in ancient Athens. When there was a vote in the assembly, it was usually in the form of a show of hands. But some decisions were made by casting physical votes, mainly in the courts. One method used pegs, where a hollow end indicated one view and a solid end showed the other. Sometimes small stones were dropped into urns representing different positions, which is why the Greek word for pebbles – *psephos* – gave its name to the modern study of elections, psephology.

One of the most frequent issues to be voted on was whether someone should be thrown out of the city. For this, citizens cast their vote by writing the name of their target on a shard of broken pottery, an *ostraka*. Hence, 'ostracize', the modern word for banishment. More than 8,000 of these fragments were discovered by German archaeologists in a filled-in Athenian river in the 1960s. Named the Great Kerameikos Deposit, the details were published in the 1990s and gave a roll-call of names and alleged grievances worthy of ostracism, ranging from incest to military defeat and overly ostentatious lifestyles.

That debate continued when democracy was revived centuries later. In the United Kingdom, voting was a very public event, more like a festival than the confession booth. Voters could be bribed or beaten up as they announced who they supported. One of the country's first big leaps towards modern democracy was the introduction of the secret ballot in 1872. The French Constitution of 1795 promised voting in secret, but it was not until 1913 that French voters sealed their ballot paper in an envelope before putting in a ballot box.

Compulsory votes

If casting a ballot is such a significant element of democracy, should citizens be forced to do it? Around half of the world's democracies have made it compulsory for voters to be registered, but only 13 per cent of countries compel them to vote, according to a 2021 study by the International Institute for Democracy and Electoral Assistance (International IDEA). Australia is the only English-speaking democracy where it is mandatory to turn up on election day. Initially introduced in the state of Queensland in 1915, compulsory voting was used at a national level from 1925 after turnout fell from 71 per cent to 60 per cent between 1919 and 1922.

Supporters of compulsion argue that it encourages civic engagement and lends greater legitimacy to the result. The Australian public has remained generally in favour (while simultaneously saying they would vote in similar numbers even if they were not forced to). There is a theory that left-wing parties benefit the most because their supporters are likely to turn up the least if voting is optional, but the evidence to suggest this is true is very mixed.

Australia's compulsory voting rule interacts with its preference system – where electors use numbers to rank the candidates – to create a side-effect called 'donkey voting'. This is when electors apparently cannot be bothered and so just write down the numbers next to the candidates in alphabetical order. Clearly, it benefits parties with candidates whose surnames are at the start of the alphabet. An Australian parliamentary committee recommended that compulsory voting be kept, but the preference element be made voluntary after the election of 2019. The government rejected this as an attack on the mandatory system as a whole.

The condensed idea
The act of democracy

36 Elections

A citizen, a curtain, a ballot box, a mandate. It is difficult to say when the first modern election was held because various elements have been introduced at different times. George Washington was elected head of state of the United States in 1789, but by an electoral college not directly by the public. In 1834, prior to becoming British prime minister, Robert Peel wrote the first manifesto of political promises in Tamworth, in the Midlands. The Australian state of Tasmania introduced the secret ballot in 1856.

The electoral ideal

Drafted by a French jurist, a Canadian law professor, a Chinese playwright and a Lebanese poet, all under the watchful eye of Eleanor Roosevelt, Article 21(3) of the United Nations Declaration of Human Rights made elections an essential part of the postwar settlement:

> 'The will of the people shall be the basis of the authority of government; this will shall be expressed in periodic and genuine elections which shall be by universal and equal suffrage and shall be held by secret vote or by equivalent free voting procedures.'

Ideological differences in the brewing Cold War meant that when the declaration was adopted at the UN General Assembly in Paris in 1948, several countries abstained – among them the former Soviet Union and some of its republics, some countries from eastern Europe, South Africa and Saudi Arabia.

Good or bad?

Modern political philosophers differ in their views on the value of elections, depending on whether their interpretation of democracy is 'thin' or 'thick'. Those who take the thin approach tend to agree with the Austrian political economist Joseph Schumpeter, who defined democracy as 'that institutional arrangement for arriving at political decisions in which individuals acquire the power to decide by means of a competitive struggle for the people's vote'. Just having elections is enough under Schumpeter's version of democracy, a view that is often labelled as 'minimalist'.

Terry Karl called this 'the fallacy of electoralism'. For her, and other adherents of the 'thick' definition, democracy is much more than just the holding of elections. It also includes the levels of political equality in the political system, the outcomes of government policies, and checks and balances on power, among other things. In short, for a country to count as a democracy, the presence of elections is necessary but not sufficient by itself. This distinction matters if, say, a government has a foreign policy that promotes democracy elsewhere. Which type? And with the goal of promoting elections or building institutions?

There are also differing views on whether elections have a positive or negative impact on nations for which democracy is fairly new. Jack Snyder and Edward Mansfield argued in 2008 that it could be dangerous to introduce elections too soon after the downfall of a dictatorship. Their statistical analysis found that a country with an

The median voter

Former German Chancellor Angela Merkel campaigned for the 2007 election in front of a slogan Die Mitte – the middle – and claimed: 'We are here in the middle – and only we'. She was making a moral point about avoiding extremes, but also referencing the potent political theory of the 'median voter'. In 1948 the Scottish economist Duncan Black proved that voters in the middle of the political spectrum usually chose the side that ended up winning. This meant that political parties who wanted to win tended to converge on this point in terms of their policies. An age of more polarized politics has called the theory into question. And there are many other ways of conceptualizing how elections work. Are they meant to capture public opinion and turn it into policy, the so-called 'aggregative model'? Or, in Joseph Schumpeter's view, are they really just fights between elites played out on the battlefield of public opinion?

'incomplete' democratic transition was twice as likely to have a civil war than an autocracy. By studying post-election conflict in Burundi, Indonesia, Peru, Argentina and elsewhere, they concluded that elections could unleash ethnic, religious, economic or factional forces that erupted in violence. Better to wait for strong institutions to form before rushing the population to the polls, Snyder and Mansfield concluded.

But in 2011 Swedish academic Staffan Lindberg looked at 232 elections in 44 African countries between 1989 and 2003. He found that the fact an election was happening was more important than whether it was fought fairly or in perfect conditions. In other words, a slightly corrupt election was better than no election at all. For Lindberg, three was the magic number because that was how many consecutive contests it took for democracy to become entrenched. Behaving democratically helped democracy become established, he argued.

The electoral cycle

The Council of Europe and the International Institute for Democracy and Electoral Assistance (IDEA) have made an attempt to boil down the countless electoral rules and traditions around the world. Their model of the classic electoral cycle is split into eight steps that take place in three phases.

The pre-election phase includes the laws that underpin the election and other rules, such as the drawing of constituency boundaries or the thresholds above which parties need to poll to be elected or the limits on financial contributions, depending on the type of electoral system that is used. This has led Harvard expert on elections Pippa Norris to reject the use of the term 'electoral manipulation' because the presence of rules mean all elections are manipulated to a certain extent. This phase ends with the election campaign, the length of which varies from place to place. The 2020 US presidential election technically lasted for 1,194 days; Australia has a minimum campaign period of 33 days; the official campaign for the Japanese parliamentary election is just 12 days. The second phase is the election itself and the verification of the results. Then comes the post-election phase, which throughout history has ended variously in the status quo, the peaceful handover of power between governments, political violence or the result being challenged in court.

The condensed idea
Necessary but not sufficient for democracy?

37 Voting Systems

Studying the different voting systems used throughout the world can be like reading a wine list – subtle differences only fully appreciable by experts, and a lot of exotic names, such as d'Hondt, Droop, Hagenbach-Bischoff and Webster/Sainte-Laguë. But, like wine, there are some broad categories:

Majoritarian This winner is the candidate who gets at least 50 per cent of the votes, plus one. Under a plurality system, it is the candidate who receives the most votes, which might not be a majority and may be quite a lot less than 50 per cent. The choice can be made in one go (British Members of Parliament) or over several rounds of voting (the French president) or can happen *within* the ballot paper, when electors indicate preferences among several candidates, known as an instant run-off or the Alternative Vote (Australia).

Proportional representation In proportional systems, the seats in the legislature reflect the parties' share of the vote, depending on which of several formulas a country has chosen. Often this means citizens vote for political parties, and the person who ends up representing them comes from a list of candidates chosen by the parties (the Netherlands). 'Top-up' seats can be used to compensate for quirks in the system, or to address inequalities. An alternative proportional system is the single transferrable vote, where voters rank their candidates in order of preference and as candidates are eliminated during the counting process, the preferences of their voters are allocated to others (Ireland). Systems can be 'mixed' because they use a combination of different methods (New Zealand), or because voters elect a mixture of candidates *and* parties (also New Zealand).

Which system a country uses is a product of history, geography and power shifts between political parties. The Spanish political scientist Carles Boix identified three eras. The first was before the introduction of universal suffrage, when majority systems dominated. Then came the expansion of the franchise either side of the First World War, which created new types of party representing new types of voter.

They demanded new types of electoral system, which gave them more chance of winning. This was followed by a period of stability in electoral systems from the 1920s. Boix argued that the main driver behind electoral reform had less to do with complaints of unfairness from the electorate or the losers and owed more to calculation by the dominant political party of how best to stay in charge.

A later example of the switch from a majoritarian to a proportional system is provided by New Zealand. There, the Labour Party promised a referendum on a new voting system in the 1980s but abandoned it after doing well under the old one. Sensing an opportunity, the rival National Party then promised the public a choice on a new system, which it was obliged to deliver after it won the next election. New Zealand moved to proportional representation in 1996. In 2011 the United Kingdom held a referendum on adopting the Alternative Vote (where a candidate has to secure at least 50 per cent of the votes). A compromise agreed during the formation of a coalition government and which pleased neither side, was rejected overwhelmingly by the public.

The weight of a vote

Some systems fail to deliver the democratic ideal of 'one person, one vote' because they appear to give greater weight to some votes over others. In the United States, Columbia University statistician Andrew Gelman crunched the results of several presidential elections state by state. Acknowledging that there were differences between elections with a close call or a landslide, and states that were evenly divided or politically polarized, Gelman found that the odds of a citizen theoretically casting the vote that decided the outcome of the election was, on average, 1 in 10 million. But this disguised big variations: from a 1 in 1.8 million chance in a state with a small population such as Alaska, to a 1 in *hundreds* of millions chance for a populous state such as California.

Because it is very unlikely there would ever be a situation in which there was a tie-break that could be decided by a single voter, Gelman and other political scientists admit that this is of limited practical value. But these thought experiments were designed to highlight genuine flaws in electoral systems. Politicians also perform real-world versions of these calculations so that they can target the swing seats that might prove decisive.

A related situation occurs in the UK's majoritarian system. A 'safe seat' is one where the incumbent party wins by a comfortable margin in each election, removing any jeopardy from the outcome and leaving the voters of other parties potentially feeling disenfranchised. Also, the Labour Party secures more votes in highly populated areas, whereas the Conservative Party performs well in less populated rural areas, meaning the former 'piles up' votes that might not be decisive, and the latter wins seats with fewer votes. At the parliamentary election in 2019, according to the House of Commons Library, this meant the number of votes required for Labour to win a seat was 50,835; for the Conservatives it was 38,264.

Social choice theory

Is voting the best way to synthesize the views of the electorate? The French mathematician Nicolas de Condorcet provided a justification for it as a means for reaching a correct decision with his jury theorem in the 18th century, but also threw a spanner in the works with his theory of majority cycles. In 1785, Condorcet proved that when more than three voters had a choice of three options, multiple majorities could be present at the same time, invalidating the very idea of a majority at all. Option A could beat B, B could beat C and C could beat A. A winning option could only be described as a 'Condorcet winner' if it beat all others after a series of two-horse races. This theory disappeared for a few centuries before being re-discovered by, among others, the English mathematician Charles Dodgson, who wrote *Alice's Adventures in Wonderland* under his pen name, Lewis Carroll.

Alice would have felt right at home in the topsy-turvy world of social choice theory that emerged as a consequence. This boomed in the 1950s after the American Nobel Prize-winning economist Kenneth Arrow coined his 'impossibility theorem'. He demonstrated that no electoral system could satisfy five criteria that you would broadly want it to (such as not giving one person the ability to have a casting vote because that effectively made them a dictator). This has spawned a section of academia that seeks the ideal way to turn the vast confusion of public opinion into valid decisions. It relies on complex equations that can feel like politics through the looking glass.

Minority democrats

In the UK contest of 2019, 15.5 million voters – around 45 per cent – voted for a candidate who lost. The Swiss philosopher Jean-Jacques Rousseau foresaw this when the wrote in *The Social Contract*, in 1762:

> 'But it is asked how a man can be both free and forced to conform to wills that are not his own. How can the opponent be both free and be placed in subjection to laws to which they have not consented?'

This has been described as the 'the paradox of the minority democrat'. In a 1962 essay, the British philosopher Richard Wollheim thought about an election where there was an option A and an option B. An imaginary voter might choose option B but accept option A as the winner because the majority had voted for it. This was a contradiction, Wollheim argued, because the voter was now simultaneously in favour of both options. Political philosophers have tended to solve this conundrum by arguing that voters find legitimacy in the act of voting, not the outcome (voting is of 'intrinsic' not 'instrumental' value in their jargon).

The condensed idea
Much more than a cross in a box

38 The Overton Window

I n the mid-1990s an electrical engineer-turned-lawyer-turned-free-markets-wonk named Ian Overton was touting for business for his Michigan-based think-tank the Mackinac Center for Public Policy. He presented clients with a list of policies on school funding. They were ranked from 'most free' at the top to 'least free' at the bottom. So, they went from 'No government policy on school attendance' to

---

Brexit?

The United Kingdom's departure from the European Union, known by the neologism Brexit, is often cited as an example of the shifting of the Overton Window. The caricature is that the United Kingdom moved from slightly uneasy membership of the bloc to the previously unimaginable break from it under the influence of charismatic politicians, such as the former leader of the UK Independence Party, Nigel Farage, who spent years nudging public opinion in that direction.

But the real story is more complicated. Public opinion about the EU had been in constant flux anyway. When Margaret Thatcher came to power, 65 per cent of voters wanted to leave the Common Market. When Tony Blair was elected, a majority wanted to stay. What really allowed Brexit to happen was a shift within the Conservative Party over what to offer the public: a referendum on a new EU Treaty then became a possible referendum on revised terms of EU membership, which then became a binary in-or-out decision.

So, was this an Overton shift? Advocates of the window theory could argue that public opinion had been changed, whereas critics would say this fails to capture the complex combination of factors that produced Brexit. David Cameron, the prime minister at the time, has maintained that the referendum was an inevitable consequence of further EU integration rather than a reaction of his to political pressure.

'All students must attend federally controlled schools'. In the middle were suggestions such as 'Students may choose any [state] school in any district' and 'Private schooling publicly funded with vouchers or tax credits.'

Overton presented the policies as a vertical list to get away from the idea of a political spectrum spanning left and right. (Although the suggestions at the top do seem quite right wing and those at the bottom more left leaning). He then moved a cardboard slider with a cellophane window up and down the list to illustrate that public opinion tended to favour a cluster of policies at any one time. 'The window of political possibility', he called it. The job of think-tanks and campaigners, he argued, was to shift the window up or down the list to make previously fringe policies appear more mainstream.

Overton died in 2003 in an ultralight aircraft crash. It was only after his death that his colleagues at the Mackinac Center gave his name to the tool he had created. Nowadays they promote it as a product on their website with videos, case studies, Q&As and testimonials, as if it were toothpaste or travel insurance. They give the Prohibition-era United States as the classic example of a shift in the Overton Window: worries that the Roaring Twenties were too raucous led to a total ban on alcohol, which was then deemed too draconian and that now seems ridiculous (to liberal, Western ears at least).

Politicians look, not lead

The Mackinac Center asserts strongly, that politicians have very little power to shift the Overton Window. 'Politicians will rarely feel free to put in place whatever policy they choose at any time they choose; rather, they will calculate that their range of choices is shaped by the ideas that drive social movements and societal sensibilities', the think-tank's director Joseph Lehman blogged. He argues there are only two types of leader who ignore the consequences of the window: visionaries, who are very rare . . . and losers.

The concept is so compelling and so simple that observers claim to see it in operation everywhere, from shifting attitudes to climate change, same-sex marriage, Islam and even in a social media exchange around fans' feelings about the *Star Wars* films. It also has a whiff of a grand theory that explains everything – the revelation of some hidden

A distant cousin of the Overton Window that similarly appears to reveal some of the mysteries of the democratic process, but from a different angle, is voter segmentation. This is when the electorate is broken down into discrete groups so that political messages can be better targeted.

The technique became famous during the 1996 presidential election campaign between Bill Clinton and Bob Dole, when a Republican campaign strategist named Alex Castellanos described a type of voter being wooed by the Democrats as the 'soccer mom'. She was 'the overburdened middle-income working mother who ferries her kids from soccer practice to scouts to school,' Castellanos said. This tactic was pioneered by an opinion pollster who worked for the Clintons, Mark Penn. Over the years the soccer mom was joined by the 'security mom' and the 'ice hockey mom'. Organizations have added 'bro-publicans', 'disengaged battlers' and 'comfortable nostalgists'. Research by the campaign group More in Common in 2018 found that the largest group of voters in the United States was 'the exhausted majority'.

wiring in society. That feeling was given a boost when *Fox News* anchor Glenn Beck wrote a conspiracy novel called *The Overton Window* in 2010.

A mutated Overton Window?

Critics complain that the theory underplays the agency of politicians and claim there is a lack of evidence to prove its existence. And there is suspicion around its origin as a publicity tool for a think-tank that raises money to argue for a smaller state. 'Political homeopathy', is how one British political commentator described it. The American progressive campaigner Sean McElwee refers instead to 'going through the "Overton Door"', where politicians alter public opinion over time by incremental policy changes. In other words, do not go for a big-bang overhaul of healthcare but instead pass laws that change the system piecemeal and get states to make changes that build momentum towards doing things another way. He also warns that provocative policies designed to shift the window can backfire and become millstones around the necks of those who proposed them.

Others say that the original concept is being misused, and that very provocative ideas are publicized to make previously quite provocative ideas look more acceptable. Many American commentators give Donald Trump's rhetoric on immigration as an example of this on the right and the Defund the Police campaign on the left. The promoter of the original concept Joseph Lehman agreed when he told an interviewer: 'Journalists or pundits sometimes treat the Overton Window as if it is a tool designed for the purpose of manipulation, and that's not what it's for. It's like saying, gravity is for the purpose of dropping pianos on people's heads.'

Like all successful metaphors about politics, the Overton Window sounds neat but only gets you so far in describing the real world.

The condensed idea
The art of the politically possible

39 Federalism

Federalism is used to manage national or religious differences within a state. According to the Ottawa-based Forum for Federations, around 40 per cent of the world's population live in the 25 countries that could be described as 'federal'. But each one has applied a unique recipe that is a product of their mixture of regional identities, geography, history and politics. Federalism is different in the United States, Canada, India, Australia, Germany and Nigeria, making it difficult to summarize.

Broadly it is an arrangement for governing where power is shared between several territorial units of a country and wielded at multiple levels – national, regional and local. It requires processes for the allocation of powers and public money. The rules are usually written down in a constitution, which is umpired by a supreme judicial body. In a 'symmetrical' federation, each unit has the same powers; in an 'asymmetric' federation some units have more powers than others.

The ultimate federation

Federations – or the looser form, confederations – existed among the tribes of Israel, the settlements of ancient Greece and the city-states of Renaissance Italy and the Netherlands. But the modern form was created in Philadelphia in 1787, when the delegates at the constitutional convention decided to turn the United States from a confederation of former colonies into a formal federal system.

The drafting process was about balancing the rights of the states against the powers of the new central government. The end product was the Constitution. Promoting the document to the public, future president, James Madison, pitched the new structure as a mixture of elements that were national (Congress, the presidency and the Supreme Court) and federal (which preserved the powers and identities of the states).

The proposed Constitution, therefore, is in strictness neither a national nor a federal Constitution but a composition of both.
James Madison, 1788

This was achieved by limiting Congress to passing only the 'necessary and proper' laws required so that the federal government could carry out the small number of tasks it had been given. These included the management of trade between states and with other countries, minting money, declaring war, setting up the post office, and providing for the 'general welfare' of the young country.

This has meant that each state has retained its own government, legislature and supreme court, often with their own rules, such as term limits for elected officials. Hence why a governor of Wisconsin can run for re-election again and again, but can serve only once in Virginia. The states have retained powers over many areas of life, from education to crime and civil law. This is why prostitution is legal in Nevada, but nowhere else; why marijuana is permitted in more than 20 states but not all; why the state of California could introduce tougher emissions standards for cars than most others. Schools are usually funded from local taxes, leading to wide educational inequalities.

But the big story of American federalism has been the expansion of the powers of the national institutions. Partly this is because modern life requires more inter-state commerce (think flying, the internet, banking) but this centralization has also been driven by rulings of the Supreme Court and by political decisions, frequently over the spending of federal funds.

The Supreme Court The judgment in the case of Ware v Hylton (1796) established that treaties signed by the federal government took precedence over agreements made by the states. This nullified a law in Virginia and established for the first time that state law was trumped by federal law. Many other landmark rulings followed over hundreds of years, for example Obergefell v Hodges (2015), when judges ruled that all states had to recognize same-sex marriage because citizens were entitled to 'equal protection' from the law under the 14th amendment to the Constitution.

Political decisions States are dependent on federal government funds for around 30 per cent of their income. This gives the national institutions substantial leverage. For example, some federal highways funds are linked to whether a state enforces the law on seat belts.

Buckle up or lose out. The federal government has also issued 'mandates' – laws that apply equally across the country, such as The Clean Water Act and The Americans with Disabilities Act.

In a way, all debates in American politics are about the definition of what is 'necessary and proper' for Congress to maintain the appropriate division between the states and the federal government on the issues of the day, whether this is the size of the national debt, the right to access abortion, or energy policy in the face of climate change. The pros and cons of federalism in the United States apply in all federations. Is it a guarantee of stability or a recipe for gridlock? Protection of diversity or a driver of polarization? A way to experiment

Quasi-federations

The United Kingdom is technically a unitary state but with some semi-federal twists, which the British prefer to label 'devolution'. The constituent nations of Scotland, Wales and Northern Ireland have a Parliament, Senedd and Assembly respectively, and their own executives. Processes for managing the relationships have often ended up with the names of the men who invented them, including the Sewel convention, which is supposed to stop UK Parliament from legislating in an area of competence of the Scottish government without consulting the Scots first, and the Barnett formula, which defines the allocation of public spending to the devolved institutions. Despite the numerical dominance of English MPs in the House of Commons, England does not have its own specific representation in the system. One outcome has been a heated debate about whether there should be 'English votes for English laws'.

A federal structure manages the union between the seven members of the United Arab Emirates, but each emirate has its own royal family and retains so much power that some describe the UAE as more of a confederation.

with different policies in different places, or a source of duplication and inefficiency as different units have to deliver the same things? Sometimes federalism is all of these at the same time.

Failed federations

Federations have sometimes failed. The former Czechoslovakia was created as a unitary state from elements of the Austro-Hungarian Empire after the First World War. Roughly a third of its population were Slovaks in the East, the rest were Czechs in the West. In 1968 President Alexander Dubcek introduce a federal system, but its operation was severely limited under Soviet control. The country was run as a federation after communism fell in 1989, but tensions rose, making it impossible to form a government that had the support of politicians from both the Czech and Slovak communities. Without a referendum – and in spite of opinion polls that suggested there was public support for staying together – members of parliament voted for a split. A process known as the 'velvet divorce' created Slovakia and the Czech Republic on 1st January 1993. (The Czech Republic renamed itself Czechia in 2016.)

Pakistan emerged as a federation from the partition of India in 1947, albeit one where its two units were separated by language, culture and thousands of miles. The union between East and West Pakistan collapsed in 1971 after a two-week civil war. This led to the birth of Bangladesh as an independent country, and provided another example where federalism struggled to contain tensions rather than manage them, disproving the main advantage that is attributed to federalist models.

The condensed idea
Power shared

40 Accountability

The time at which elected representatives are most accountable is in an election. But several other tools can be used – in the words of a foul-mouthed but famous Australian phrase – 'to keep the b*****ds honest'.

Impeachment

One of the most powerful procedures is the removal of a head of state or government from office before either an election or the constitutionally mandated end of their term. This is impeachment.

Thanks to presidents Nixon, Clinton and Trump, the impeachment process the world is most familiar with is in the United States. According to the Constitution, an American president can be impeached if they can be shown to have committed 'treason, bribery, or other high crimes and misdemeanors'. To be impeached technically means facing a vote in the Senate that could result in removal from office.

In the United States, the process begins with a vote in the House of Representatives, which then moves to the upper chamber. Although the Chief Justice of the Supreme Court presides over an impeachment trial, events are held in the Senate rather than the court because there are more senators than judges, and in the words of Alexander Hamilton '[the] awful discretion which a court of impeachments must necessarily have, to doom to honor or infamy the most confidential and the most distinguished characters of the community forbids the commitment of the trust to a small number of persons.' The Constitution demands a two-thirds majority to remove a president from office.

Andrew Johnson faced impeachment in 1868, but escaped conviction by one vote. Two motions of impeachment were passed against Bill Clinton in 1998, over his handling of his affair with the White House intern Monica Lewinsky, but neither received the super-majority required to remove him. Donald Trump faced impeachment on two separate occasions – over claims he pressurized the Ukrainian government to investigate Joe Biden's son and over the January 6 riots at the Capitol. Neither vote crossed the two-thirds threshold, but the second saw seven Republicans voting against the president, the highest number of senators opposing 'their own side' in the history of impeachments. The only time a president has left the White House because of an impeachment was in 1973, when Richard Nixon resigned before his Senate trial.

America has monopolized the coverage of the process but not its existence. Impeachment features in the constitutions of most countries with a presidential system. Research suggests that a quarter of national leaders faced impeachment between the 1970s and the early 2000s.

In 2023, Ecuador tried out a new clause in its constitution, which is nicknamed *muerte cruzada* – 'mutual death'. This means that if the National Assembly votes to impeach the president or the president dissolves the assembly, then both branches of government are subject to fresh elections at the same time. The measure was designed to prevent the back-and-forth impeachments and dissolutions of the legislature that had characterized Ecuadorian political life.

Impeachment: cause and effect

In 2021, American academics Tom Ginsburg, Aziz Huq and David Landau published the first statistical study of impeachment attempts from around the world. They backed up the empirical data with deep dives into impeachment proceedings in the United States, South Korea, Brazil, Paraguay and South Africa. The trio found that the procedure was used less to deal with criminality and more often to handle a dramatic loss of support for the president among their people. Claims of criminality were sometimes present (such as in the case of Park Geun-hye of South Korea) but they were almost always accompanied by a political crisis around the leader. The research also suggested that an impeachment had little or no effect on the performance of a democracy afterwards. This appeared to disprove one of the main criticisms of the process: that it is destabilizing for a country. But it apparently proved another: impeachments are acts of politics, not law.

Recall

Another means of replacing an elected representative is through a 'recall' procedure. How these play out depends on the type of official they apply to, whether they are triggered by the public or in other circumstances, if an incumbent can run in the succeeding election and other constitutional rules, such as a minimum level of voter turnout.

All of this featured in the 2003 recall vote in California, which saw Arnold Schwarzenegger become governor. The Democrat Gray Davis had been elected a year earlier, with 47 per cent of the vote. But a campaign group fighting for lower taxes gathered the signatures of more than 1.5 million Californians, many more than the 12 per cent of the state's population legally required to trigger a recall. Under the state's constitution, the decision to throw out a governor and the election of a replacement are rolled into one, with the incumbent barred from standing again. Davis lost the recall vote by 55.4 to 44.6 per cent. Arnie beat his new Democrat opponent by 48.6 to 31.5 per cent, securing a slightly larger share of the vote than Davis had in his election. Political history was made, along with a thousand and one *Total Recall* jokes.

A recall mechanism for UK Members of Parliament was introduced in the House of Commons in 2015 after a series of political scandals. If parliament's disciplinary committee recommends a suspension from office of more than 10 sitting days, or an MP commits a serious crime, then constituents can sign a petition requesting a recall. If

Monitoring money

Many parliaments have searchable registers of members' financial arrangements. This is how journalists could calculate that the former British Prime Minister Boris Johnson earned £5m in less than a year after he left office. There are often rules about expenses and allowances, and about relationships with outside employers and interests. US Congress approved the Ethics in Government Act for all public officials in 1978, following the Watergate scandal. It limits the amount members of Congress and the House of Representatives can earn outside politics to a maximum of 15 per cent of their congressional salary, for example.

more than 10 per cent do so, then a by-election is called, where the incumbent can stand again. Mayors can be recalled in Germany. Local politicians can be recalled in British Columbia. Officials up to, and including, the president can be recalled in Venezuela.

Ethics frameworks

Different political systems have developed other formal and informal ethics mechanisms. Some have codes of conduct that specify to varying degrees the behaviour expected of parliamentarians, both generally and in the chamber of the legislature. Following the so-called 'cash-for-questions' scandal of 1990, the United Kingdom adopted seven 'Nolan principles' for public life, named after Lord Nolan, who chaired the committee that drafted them. They are: selflessness, integrity, objectivity, accountability, openness, honesty and leadership. Each incoming prime minister updates the Ministerial Code, which governs the behaviour of members of the government. The fact that the prime minister remains the code's ultimate arbiter has led to accusations that they play the role of judge, jury and executioner of their own colleagues.

The condensed idea
Keeping them honest

41 Populism

There are three problems when considering the concept of populism. The first is that all politicians are populists in a sense because they need the support of enough people to be elected. Experts in the field would say this is an incorrect use of the term and that 'populist' applies to a specific type of politician or movement that claims to represent 'the people' in a battle against 'the elite'.

But this leads to the second problem: the word has proved difficult to define. The academic Cas Mudde has attempted to solve this by referring to populism as a 'thin-centred' ideology – that is, less a set of core beliefs as with capitalism, socialism or nationalism and more like an attitude. Others use 'populist' as an adjective to talk about a set of political techniques, such as the undermining of the independent judiciary. The third issue is that the term is often used as an insult by politicians and observers who feel under threat from the forces they label as 'populist', making discussions about it feel very loaded.

The earliest populists

The election of the world's most famous and most powerful populist, Donald Trump, as president of the United States in 2016, along with Jair Bolsonaro's presidency in Brazil and Viktor Orbán's leadership of Hungary, has meant that modern populism has often been characterized as nationalist, anti-immigrant and of the right. But its earlier expressions were much more left-leaning.

The word 'populism' originated in 19th-century Russia, with the narodnichestvo movement, which was translated into English as 'going to the people'. The *narod* were the country's agricultural workers. Power rightfully belonged in their hands, according to a group of urban intellectuals, who would visit rural communities wearing labourers' clothes and urge their rural compatriots to overthrow the aristocracy. The original organization split and one of its successors, People's Will, assassinated Tsar Alexander II in 1881.

The countryside was also the focus of the first populist movement in the United States. The People's Party was formed by farmers in the western states. It met on 4 July 1892 to adopt a set of policies called the Omaha Platform. These included a more progressive income tax and the production of more silver coins. These 'prairie populists' wanted the railways to be taken over by the government and for unused land owned by the railroad companies to be redistributed to the people.

Latin American populists

It was in South America that populist sentiment was most effectively translated into government. Following the economic turbulence of the Great Depression in 1929, populists came to power in Brazil, Ecuador and Argentina. The last was led by the husband and wife who became the very definition of Latin American populism – Juan and Eva Perón. From 1946, they showered the *descamisados* – 'the shirtless' poor – with cash, as immortalized in the Andrew Lloyd Weber and Tim Rice musical, *Evita*. A modern populist wave began on the continent in 1998 with the election of Hugo Chávez in Venezuela, before spreading to Bolivia (led

> Let the enemies of the people, of Perón and the Fatherland come. I have never been afraid of them because I have always believed in the people.
>
> Eva Perón, on the balcony of the Casa Rosada, October 1951

Caudillismo

'Caudillo' – from the Spanish word for leader – was the label given to a collection of macho presidents who emerged when South American countries declared independence from the Spanish empire at the beginning of the 19th century. The phrase caudillismo has since been used to describe a range of Latin American leadership types from military dictators to former farmers, on the left and right. It conjours the image of the 'strong man', which is another common feature of populism: highly personalized leadership by a charismatic figure who has a direct link with the people, allowing institutions to be by-passed. This gendered term ignores female leaders such as Eva Perón in Argentina and Marine Le Pen in France.

by Evo Morales), Ecuador (Rafael Correa) and Nicaragua (Daniel Ortega). These regimes were characterized by state ownership of resources and antagonism towards the United States.

At the dawn of the 21st century, a wave of populism appeared to sweep across the continent of Europe but because its movements were based on different grievances, it was more varied than earlier incarnations. The increasing number of powers handed to the EU by national governments helped eurosceptics, such as the United Kingdom Independence Party (UKIP), make the case that national sovereignty was being eroded. The financial crisis led to mass youth unemployment in Spain, boosting the Podemos party. The Eurozone crisis in Greece, which required large bailouts from Brussels (with tough strings attached), led to the election of a left-wing populist government, Syriza. The migrant crisis of 2015, which saw more than a million refugees cross the Mediterranean and Aegean seas and settle in Germany, helped the anti-immigrant Alternative for Germany (AfD) party grow from 0 per cent to a peak of 20 per cent in the polls in spring 2023 – the same level as the venerable Social Democrat Party (SPD).

Responses

Europeans have adopted various policies to constrain the power of populist movements when they have been perceived as a threat to democracy. In Germany, the Federal Office for the Protection of the Constitution has placed elements of the anti-immigrant AfD under surveillance. On the eve of elections in 2023, the head of the domestic intelligence service warned that voting for the party was a risk to national security. The *cordon sanitaire* – sanitary cordon – was an agreement among the mainstream parties in Belgium to refuse to share power with the Flemish nationalist Vlaams Blok movement, which was considered to be racist. Germany's equivalent of this for the AfD is the so-called *Brandmauer* or 'firewall'.

In their 'toolkit' for combating populism, published in 2020, Andrea-Kendall Taylor and Carisa Nietsche of the think-tank the Center for New American Security rejected the firewall approach and suggested that mainstream parties consider coalitions with populist parties, as long as they met certain conditions. This could be a way to incorporate into the democratic process the genuine grievances held by the public that had been uncovered by the populist movements. Other research has suggested the traditional politicians succeed when they focus on their own issues rather than amplifying their populist challengers' causes, such as immigration.

The chronicler of British populism, Professor Matthew Goodwin of Kent University, said the elite in the United Kingdom is now comprised of graduates from top universities who have imposed 'radically progressive cultural values' on the rest of the population. He was criticized in newspaper columns and on social media by journalists, academics and campaigners who felt uncomfortable being described as part of this class. Perhaps the ultimate irony about the difficult-to-define word 'populism' is that anyone who uses it in conversation is likely to be part of the group that is being challenged.

The condensed idea
The people v the elite

42 Climate

I n the 1970s, British biochemist Professor James Lovelock made an early contribution to thinking on climate change when he proposed the Gaia hypothesis, which depicted Earth as a self-regulating system. By 2010 Lovelock had become concerned that the world's political system was failing to tackle the problem of a warming planet. 'Even the best democracies agree that when a major war approaches, democracy must be put on hold for the time being. I have a feeling that climate change may be an issue as severe as a war. It may be necessary to put democracy on hold for a while,' he told the *Guardian* newspaper.

Environmentalists against democracy

Proponents of this view – the extreme version of which has been described as 'eco-authoritarianism' by its critics – argue that democracy prevents action against climate change because it inevitably leads to compromise, not radical action. For example, the Green Party in Germany has had to water down its ambitious pledges as part of a coalition government with the Social Democrats. The freedom of speech inherent to modern democracy gives sceptics access to the airwaves to cast doubt on the scientific evidence, which can be seized up by vested interests to resist change and give confused voters an excuse not to care.

Changes in government result in changes to policy, which creates inconsistency. Take US membership of the Paris Agreement on climate change: signed by Barack Obama in 2015, rescinded by Donald Trump in 2017, re-joined by Joe Biden in 2021. The need for politicians to get re-elected also makes it difficult for them to do unpopular things. Opposition to onshore wind turbines in rural England led the British Conservative government to ban their construction, shifting the focus to offshore windfarms, which were more expensive but less visible to voters.

China is cited as proof of these contentions. Its record on solar power is an example: in 2023 China will produce eight out of ten of the world's solar panels, and will install in one year the same volume of solar capacity as the United States has installed since the 1970s.

Environmental democrats

However, in 2021 the V-Dem project in Gothenburg, which collects authoritative data on the world's political systems, published 'robust empirical evidence' that it said proved the superiority of democracies over authoritarian regimes when it came to climate policies. The Swedish analysts found that democracies generally had more ambitious commitments to reduce carbon emissions and were more likely to have signed international climate change agreements. Countries that were more equal and less corrupt had better air quality. The presence of civil society organizations, such as campaign groups, was also a predictor of lower carbon emissions. Overall, a 10 per cent increase in V Dem's democratic indicators led to a 3 per cent reduction in CO_2, the academics concluded.

Activists have used democratic institutions, especially the courts, to force governments to improve their climate policies. A seminal moment was the case of Neubauer, et al v Germany in 2021, when the German Constitutional Court in Karlsruhe found against the government and in favour of young campaigners from the Fridays for the Future movement, which was started by the Swedish activist Greta Thunberg. The judges ruled that the German climate law was unconstitutional because most of the cuts to carbon emissions were pencilled in for after 2030. Meeting the target meant potentially draconian curbs on the freedoms of future generations which, the judges unanimously agreed, was a breach of the constitution. The German government brought forward a new law with earlier cuts.

The Sabin Center at Columbia Law School maintains a database of climate change litigation and has counted 2,341 cases worldwide, two-thirds of which have been filed since the passage of the Paris Agreement. In 2022 countries such as Turkey and Russia saw their first climate-related legal challenges.

Climate governance

Tackling climate change has led to the creation of a new type of transnational democracy, captured by the umbrella term 'climate governance'. In 1992 world leaders created the United Nations Framework Convention on Climate Change (UNFCC) that kickstarted regular global summits on climate change, some of which were deemed successful (Kyoto in 1997) or disastrous (Copenhagen in 2009).

Collective action

Climate change is often described as a 'collective action problem'. This is the phenomenon where individuals have an incentive to act selfishly rather than cooperating with others, even when a joint solution could benefit everyone. It is often illustrated by the prisoner's dilemma – a thought experiment where prisoners in neighbouring cells are offered the opportunity to help each other but betray their fellow inmate instead.

The Scottish philosopher David Hume spotted the problem in 1738 when he wrote that two people could probably work out how to drain a meadow but it was unlikely – probably impossible – 'that a thousand persons should agree in any such action; it being difficult for them to concert so complicated a design, and still more difficult for them to execute it; while each seeks a pretext to free himself of the trouble and expense, and would lay the whole burden on others.' The idea was expanded upon in the 1960s by the American politicial scientist Mancur Olson in his book *The Logic of Collective Action*, which also popularized the idea of 'the free rider' – someone who gets the benefits without any of costs. The Paris Agreement on climate change was designed to create a virtuous circle of ever-increasing ambition and sought to overcome the problem of winners and losers.

This eventually led to the signing of the 2015 Paris Agreement, which committed governments to limit the overall increase in the average temperature of the planet to 'well below' 2 degrees by the end of the 21st century, and ideally to no more than 1.5 degrees. Countries would do this by making pledges to reduce their carbon emissions – so-called 'nationally determined contributions'. These would be updated annually at meetings called Conferences of the Parties (COP), with an aspiration that these targets would become more ambitious every year.

The COP process was designed to create a level playing field between countries large and small, rich and poor, those that have benefitted the most economically from carbon-intensive industries and those that have not but are already feeling the effects of a changing climate. The flaws in this grand experiment in international democracy were apparent in the closing moments of the 26th COP meeting in Glasgow in December 2021. Minutes before a painstakingly negotiated final text was to be signed off, delegates from China, India and the United States huddled behind closed doors. They emerged with a rewrite of the language on fossil fuels. They had replaced the phrase 'phasing out' with 'phasing down'. This last-minute manouvering left diplomats from smaller countries fuming and the British chair of the conference in tears. At the other end of the scale, climate activists argue that the tools of direct democracy, such as citizens assemblies, are necessary to secure consent for the lifestyle changes that will be required to manage a warming planet.

> **We have to look forward not backward and we shall only succeed in dealing with the problems through a vast international, cooperative effort.**
> Margaret Thatcher to the United Nations, November 1989

The condensed idea
A big challenge for democracy

43 Direct Action

There was an addition to the regular sporting calendar in the British summer of 2023: very visible protestors. An activist from Just Stop Oil exploded orange powder over a table at the World Snooker Championships. Another was carried off the pitch when England's cricketers were playing Australia in the Ashes. Animal rights campaigners were accused of contributing to the death of racehorses when they delayed the start of the Grand National. These events were examples of direct action, a set of techniques outside the formal political process designed to create political change. But direct action is also an intellectual and historical tradition that goes beyond powder bombs and pitch invasions.

Non-violence

Tolstoy is often cited as inspiration. His work *The Kingdom of God is Within You*, a reference to the biblical verse Luke 17:21, was published in Germany in 1894. The author of *War and Peace* interpreted the Christian command to 'turn the other cheek' as an instruction never to fight back. Tolstoy exchanged letters with Mohandas Gandhi when he was a lawyer fighting for human rights in South Africa in the early 20th century. Gandhi's later fight against the British for Indian independence was founded on the principle of non-violence, as seen in his call for Indians to spin their own cloth rather than buying from the United Kingdom and his famous march to the sea that culminated in him picking up a handful of salt to protest against a British tax.

Despite some of Gandhi's other views, which have since been questioned, he provided inspiration for the marches, strikes and boycotts of the American civil rights struggle of the 1950s and 60s. Martin Luther King wrote: 'I came to see for the first time that the Christian doctrine of love operating through the Gandhian method of non-violence was one of the most potent weapons available to oppressed people in their struggle for freedom.'

The techniques used by these movements, and in other non-violent struggles, such as the opposition to Communism in Eastern Europe, were collated by the academic Gene Sharp in his essay 'From Dictatorship to Democracy', written in 1994 to help campaigners against the military regime in Burma. Photocopies and smuggled editions were then used by activists in Serbia, Indonesia and in the Arab Spring. Sharp listed 198 separate direct actions under different headings. 'Symbolic public acts' includes Number 19 'wearing of symbols' and Number 26 'paint as protest'. Actions by Consumers features Number 74 'rent withholding'. Numbers 162–167 in Physical Interventions are 'sit-in, stand-in, ride-in, wade-in, mill-in, and pray-in'. Sometimes passiveness – not doing something – could be a powerful tool. Although his work is aimed at toppling dictators, it has become a textbook for protestors on many different issues.

Violence and civil disobedience

Sharp advised against the use of force because that was where the authorities were strongest, not weakest. But some direct activists believe violence is necessary and often cite a 1912 essay by the American feminist and activist Voltairine de Cleyre. She was named by her parents after the French poet Voltaire. De Cleyre argued that violence had been justified at many points in American history, such as the Boston Tea Party and to protect the Underground Railroad, which freed slaves. During a wave of industrial action and in the wake of the fatal bombing of the offices of the *Los Angeles Times*, de Cleyre wrote:

> 'Everybody smiles when union officials protest their organizations to be peaceable and law-abiding, because everybody knows they are lying. They know that violence is used, both secretly and openly; and they know it is used because the strikers cannot do any other way . . . The people in general understand that they do these things through the harsh logic of a situation which they did not create, but which forces them to these attacks in order to make good in their struggle to live or else go down the bottomless descent into poverty, that lets Death find them in the poorhouse hospital, the city street, or the river-slime.'

Less extreme than violence but higher up the scale than purely passive resistance is the idea of civil disobedience. This is when laws are broken, either to draw attention to the cause supported by the lawbreaker or to highlight the perceived injustice of the law in the first place. The label was first used by the American anarchist Henry Thoreau in 1849 when he refused to pay federal income tax as a protest against slavery.

Living the change

Often, those engaging in direct action are doing it to illustrate the new type of society they wish to create. This can be summed up in the slogan of 'be the change you want to see', which is often attributed to Gandhi but which he never said. In academic jargon this is referred to as 'pre-figurative' politics. The phrase was coined by the American political scientist Carl Boggs in 1977, when he contrasted Marxist movements that wanted to seize the levers of power with anarchist groups that practised 'forms of social relations, decision-making, culture, and human experience that are the ultimate goal.' This was put another way by the late David Graeber, the philosophical father of the anti-capitalist Occupy movement formed after the global financial crisis, when he wrote: 'At its most elaborate, the structure of one's own act becomes a kind of micro-utopia, a concrete model for one's vision of a free

A crackdown on direct action

Amnesty International launched a campaign in 2022 called 'Protect the Protest!' The human rights group argued there was a global trend by governments to crack down on peaceful protests. They said protestors were being increasingly treated as a security threat to be handled by the military, using force. New laws were being introduced to criminalize peaceful acts. An example was the United Kingdom, where the government and protestors were engaged in a game of cat and mouse with new techniques being deployed then outlawed. Activists said they were justified by the climate crisis; politicians said the public were being put a risk by, for example, ambulances being delayed on blocked roads.

society.' Pre-figurative politics receives the same scepticism from opponents as all direct action: it can push the system in a certain direction if the wider public buys into it but has usually failed to overthrow the system itself.

The condensed idea
Dramatic change

44 Identity Politics

A female academic in the United Kingdom goes to court to establish a new legal precedent that criticism of trans rights is a philosophical belief that is protected by law. A state governor in the United States signs legislation that stops teachers mentioning homosexuality in the classroom, reminiscent of similar policies in Poland and Hungary. A drag performer reads stories to some pre-school children, while a protest and a counter-protest rage outside. Welcome to another day in the culture wars, driven by the rise in identity politics.

What is identity politics? It depends how the words are used. It can mean the actions and interests of a minority group, usually fighting for equality or justice. It has been deployed to represent the large-scale shift in how voters define themselves in the 21st century, away from economic interests and towards the expression of self. And – like the word 'woke' – the phrase can also be used as an insult.

Politics of identity

While quandaries about gender-neutral toilets, or readings by drag queens, or which statues adorn a building feel new, the intellectual basis for many of the arguments reaches back centuries, or at the very least, decades.

Sex A line can be drawn from Mary Wollstonecraft's call in 1792 'Let women share the rights', through the first, second and third waves of feminism to arrive at today's 'gender critical' attitudes, which are based on the idea that biological sex cannot be changed. The debate about the difference between sex and socially conditioned gender identity began in the 1950s. In the United Kingdom, much of the argument about trans rights centres on an inconsistency between the 2004 Gender Recognition Act and the 2010 Equality Act. While the former gives a person the right to change their legal gender, the latter permits discrimination on the basis of sex if it is for a valid purpose, which means trans women can legally be excluded from women-only spaces.

De-colonization Frantz Fanon was born in the French colony of Martinique, and combined philosophy with psychoanalysis. In his works *Black Skin, White Masks* and *The Wretched of the Earth*, published in 1952 and 1961 respectively, he presented colonialism as an act of violence against indigenous people, which destroyed their privacy, safety and mental health. The only solution, he argued, was to fight back.

Race In the 1950s and 1960s American legal scholars began developing the concepts that would become critical race theory (CRT). This was the idea that the design of the justice system was weighted in favour of white people and against black people. CRT was later extended beyond the legal sphere to all of society, to the approval of some of the theory's originators and the disapproval of others. 'White privilege' was coined in a 1989 essay by the academic Peggy McIntosh who taught at Wellesley, the women's arts college in Massachusetts. In her work on sexism, she realized that as a white person she possessed 'unearned assets' which she 'cashed in' every day, but which people of colour did not have. She listed these as if they were carried in an imaginary knapsack. These ranged from the social ('1: I can if I wish arrange to be in the company of people of my race most of the time') to the economic ('10: Whether I use cheques, credit

Intersectionality

This is the idea that people have multiple identities, which means they may experience discrimination on several levels at the same time, and even possess privilege on another. It was popularized by Kimberlé Crenshaw of Columbia Law School in an academic paper in 1989. She cited an employment case brought against a motor manufacturer, where the court ruled that black women had not been the subject of specific discrimination because the company had hired black men in some roles and white women in others. Crenshaw argued that this 'implies that the boundaries of sex and race discrimination doctrine are defined respectively by white women's and Black men's experiences. Under this view, Black women are protected only to the extent that their experiences coincide with those of either of the two groups.'

cards or cash, I can count on my skin colour not to work against the appearance of financial reliability') to the everyday ('26: I can choose blemish cover or bandages in "flesh" colour and have them more or less match my skin').

Together these theories challenged a central element of liberal democracy: that everyone was equal. Colour-blindness in public policy was blindness to people of colour, for example. Equality meant the erasure of difference.

Political identities

This shift towards expression of identity has forced political scientists to analyse voters in different ways, rather than the classic left/right or wealthy/poor split that dominated for decades. An academic who saw this coming back in the 1970s was Ronald Inglehart. In *The Silent Revolution*, he used survey data to show that since end of the Second World War, younger generations in Western democracies had shifted from security and economic concerns (which he called 'materialist') to a set of values he named 'post-materialist', more related to identity. This happened because people felt safer, and safer people could prioritize different things, such as the environment, sexual freedom and human rights. He argued that this change happened very slowly so would not reach its zenith until many years later. Older generations were not altering their views as much, which set up the potential for a backlash when they felt that society had shifted too far.

Others argue that the shift was driven by the expansion of education, by urbanization or immigration, or that a person's feeling of economic security is still the thing that defines their politics and cultural attitudes just come with it. This has led to the birth of new labels to categorize sections of the electorate in a more sophisticated way, such as the GAL-TAN scale, so-called because it places 'green, alternative, liberal' views at one end and 'traditional, authoritarian, nationalist' at the other.

Identities politicized

The consequence has been many more everyday political battles around issues of race, sex, gender, sexuality and culture, which are reported by the media and so reach a much wider group than those directly affected. This means politicians have to, at the very least, react to them, or adopt them proactively as campaign issues. This carries risks: oppose something and look reactionary and out of touch, support something and be accused of privileging one group at the expense of another, sit on the fence and risk accusations of weakness or indecision.

The historian Francis Fukuyama summarized the effect on politics in America. The left, he said, focused 'less on creating broad economic equality and more on promoting the interests of a wide variety of marginalized groups . . . The right, meanwhile, has redefined its core mission as the patriotic protection of traditional national identity.' Some would argue that the phenomenon of deep identity politics does not apply to the same extent elsewhere. The British critic Tomiwa Owolade said it with the title of his book: *This Is Not America*.

The condensed idea
It's not the economy
any more

45 Big Tech

On 14 September 2022, US senators from the House Committee on Homeland Security interrogated product designers from Twitter, YouTube, TikTok and Meta (the parent company of Facebook and Instagram). The four and a half hours of testimony summed up the interface between politics and social media. Republican members of the committee were worried about Chinese influence. Democrats were concerned about hate speech. Everyone cared about the impact on children; no one was sure how algorithms worked. The social media executives were slick and legalistic, until it came to giving basic information about how their services operated, when they were silent.

Politicians have been compelled to regulate Big Tech after a series of incidents raised public concern about its impact on society. The biggest was possibly the Cambridge Analytica (CA) scandal in 2018. The British political consultancy, which advised Donald Trump's presidential campaign among others, bought the personal data of users of an online personality quiz on Facebook called This Is Your Digital Life. This allowed CA to harvest the data of 87 million people and to use it for political purposes without their knowledge. It led to a slew of court cases, and the imposition of a US\$5 billion fine by American regulators in 2019.

> We know that this was a major violation of people's trust, and I deeply regret that we didn't do enough to deal with it.
>
> Sheryl Sandberg, Facebook Chief Operating Officer, 2018

Approaches to regulation

Tech companies initially argued that they should be allowed to regulate themselves. To fend off government intervention, at various times they have promised to hire more moderators to seek out harmful material, or given users increased options for how they interact with the services, or appointed independent oversight boards staffed by former prime ministers. But new laws are gradually being introduced to regulate online content and the flow of information that is crucial to the functioning of society.

The European Union

The EU prides itself on being an early adopter of online regulation. In 2011 it introduced the law that means users have to approve cookies when they visit a website. This was followed in 2018 by a big piece of privacy legislation, the General Data Protection Regulation (GDPR), which is why companies have to seek the consent of their users before sending them marketing emails. European officials preferred voluntary regulation of content but responded to pressure from campaigners and the public for more robust oversight. This came in 2022 with the so-called Digital Services Act package. This labelled services with more than 45 million monthly users in the EU as Very Large Online Platforms (VLOPs) or Very Large Online Search Engines (VLOSEs). This compelled companies such as Twitter and Google to publish risk assessments with policies for preventing harm to their users, especially children, and gave officials in Brussels and the EU member states more powers to intervene. This could have a potentially global impact because of the 'Brussels effect' where new EU regulations end up applying outside Europe because it makes sense for businesses to adopt the rules of their biggest market everywhere.

The United Kingdom

The United Kingdom's Online Safety Bill began its passage through Parliament in March 2022, three years after the government first proposed it. The new law would give the British communications regulator OFCOM the power to regulate social media companies, alongside TV and radio stations. The big legal shift is that it would give the owners of social media companies a 'duty of care' to their users, opening the way for criminal proceedings if harm was caused. The biggest political controversy around the legislation was a provision that gave government ministers the ability to define a category of online content that was 'legal but harmful'. Ministers said they needed a future-proof power to deal with material that fell within a grey area; advocates for free speech argued it was government intrusion and this section was dropped after much political wrangling.

The United States

The First Amendment to the constitution guarantees the right to free speech. But this does not apply to online content. Instead, it is governed by Section 230 of the Communications Decency Act passed by Congress in 1996, in the early days of the commercial internet. It says: 'No provider or user of an interactive computer service shall be treated as the publisher or speaker of any information provided by another information content provider.' This makes social media companies into platforms and not publishers, which means they escape liability for the content posted by their user. To cybersecurity expert Professor Jeff Kosseff of the US Naval Academy, these are 'the twenty-six words that invented the internet' because they allowed start-ups to flourish without the legal risks faced by newspapers or broadcasters. President Joe Biden has talked about its repeal but Congress has failed to agree how to reform it, other than the FOSTA-SESTA Act of 2018. This made some exceptions to Section 230 to prevent prostitution and sex-trafficking. It is still facing opposition from free speech advocates and sex workers. Instead, states have focused on the protection of children online leading to a patchwork of different laws.

Market dominance

Rules on internet content are fairly recent. More longstanding are attempts to control the dominance of Big Tech companies in their markets, a type of regulation known as 'anti-trust'. This dates back to the 'browser wars' of the mid-1990s where Microsoft was accused of anti-competitive practices by including its Explorer web browser in its Windows operating system. In the 2020s, anti-trust actions have tended to focus on how online marketplaces treat sellers. For instance, China has outlawed the practice of 'choose one from two', which meant vendors had to choose either of the big platforms – JD or Alibaba. The EU has taken enforcement action against Amazon and Google for how they rank some products, including their own, more highly than others. In 2022, Congress failed to pass the American Innovation and Choice Online Act (AICO), which would give US officials similar abilities and an associated law that would open up Apple and Google's app stores. But President Biden appointed regulators who vowed to use their existing powers to take a more interventionist role in managing markets in tech and other sectors.

Most of these countries have taken an approach that is described in the jargon as 'risk-based'. In other words, introducing processes to identify the possible harms posed by technologies and developing ways to mitigate them. Many campaigners would prefer something tougher and more sweeping – 'rights-based' regulation. Instead, this focuses on protecting the rights and freedoms of the individual. An example would be giving users the right to own their own data, rather than the existing situation where it is the property of the companies that are storing it. This raises the prospect of users making money from the platforms who wish to exploit the information, rather than the other way round. While regulation often combines both elements of rights and risks, this philosophical tussle will play out in a big way in the coming decade as politicians and tech companies grapple with the rise of artificial intelligence (AI).

The condensed idea
Belatedly bringing Big Tech under control

46 Electoral Integrity

T he Russian attempt to influence the 2016 US presidential contest revealed to the world the possible threats to the integrity of their elections posed by foreign governments intent on using technology to sway the opinions of voters (known by intelligence agencies as an 'influence operation') or to try to affect the electoral processes at a technical or bureaucratic level (classed as 'interference').

Mixed evidence

A 2020 report by the campaigners Freedom House said that 88 per cent of elections over two years had experienced digital interference. But this included governments taking repressive actions against their own public, such as the authorities in Myanmar shutting down the mobile phone network. A report by British parliamentarians on potential Russian meddling in UK politics released in 2020 (after a long delay) uncovered no evidence to justify allegations that the Kremlin had swung the 2016 vote on membership of the EU. But equally, it found that neither the government nor the intelligence agencies had tried very hard to find out if it had.

In March 2021, US spy agencies published a declassified report into attempts to intervene in the 2020 presidential election. They identified no efforts to interfere with the technical delivery of the vote, although Iran and Russia spread false claims that they had done this to sow doubts about the democratic process. Russia attempted to 'denigrate' candidate Biden and the Democratic Party in favour of Donald Trump but had engaged in the old-fashioned lobbying of opinion formers rather than modern online tactics. Iran's Supreme Leader Khamenei authorized an influence operation to criticize Donald Trump, in the judgment of the spooks. China thought about intervening then decided not to rock the boat. But, by their own admission, the intelligence chiefs did not reach a judgment on whether 'malign actors' in general had an impact on the outcome.

Resilience

As well as beefing up security around elections, the other main tactic used by democratic governments in the face of this threat has been to educate voters. In theory, a resilient public is less likely to fall for disinformation and more likely to trust the democratic process.

The US did this with a light-hearted leaflet about pineapple on pizza, which illustrated the first stage of a classic foreign influence operation: choosing a divisive subject. Stage two sees multiple social media accounts being created and frequently being renamed as assets are put into place. Stage three leads to existing online debates – do you like pineapple on a pizza? – being 'polluted' by trolls with extreme opinions. Stage four is an attempt to fan the flames so that the issue gets into the mainstream news – 'US gripped by debate over pizza toppings'. This culminates in stage five when the debate gets into the real world with a march in favour of pineapple and a counter-protest against it.

Watchdogs

Most countries have their own organizations to oversee elections. Some are government agencies, some are completely independent. Sometimes they can be drawn into political controversy. After the Indian election of 2019, the Indian Electoral Commission (IEC) was criticized by one group of former civil servants but defended by another.

The Canadian government introduced its Critical Election Incident Public Protocol in 2019. During an election campaign, a group of senior civil servants receive reports from the intelligence services and the political parties of any potential threats. An alert is issued to the public and candidates if a problem is serious enough.

International organizations, such as the Organization for Security and Cooperation in Europe (OSCE), usually post election observers around the world to check for old-school threats to electoral integrity, such as ballot boxes being stuffed with fake votes. For example, the parliamentary elections held in Montenegro in June 2023 were overseen by 129 officials from outside the country, including six members of the European Parliament. This meant there was one observer for every nine candidates contesting the election. The mission found the elections were 'competitive and well-run' but marked by 'populist and divisive rhetoric', the under-representation of women and there were still gaps in electoral law. Observers noted that government contracts were offered during the election period despite rules that public money could not be spent for political purposes.

Latin America's top ten election myths

In Latin America, misinformation about elections is so formulaic that the Portal Watch initiative, a product of the UN, the EU and the fact-checking service Chequeado, has produced a list of the top ten most circulated voting myths in the region. They include:

1. Irregularities in the electoral process. Pictures of paperwork with incorrect numbers of votes or crossed-out tallies are frequently circulated. Often these are provisional pieces of paperwork to assist with the counting process and not the final result.

3. Using the identification of a deceased person to vote. A video circulated during the 2021 election in Peru purporting to show a dead person's identification being used at a polling station. It was a typo, where a living voter had put a 9 instead of a 4.

5. Manipulation to prevent voting. This referred to a myth pedalled on social media in Colombia that voting was not required in the second round of the election because the voter's choice in the first round would be counted again.

7. Disinformation concerning citizens' votes in other countries. Photos circulated in Mexico of bundles of ballot papers sent to expats that appeared to have some missing. This was a product of different rules from state to state about which elections Mexicans could participate in while living abroad.

International observation missions can be controversial. Monitors, including big names such as the former US Secretary of State John Kerry, issued an endorsement of the 2017 Kenyan presidential election, the result of which was then annulled by the country's Supreme Court. Within the electoral observation community there is a debate about whether election monitors should intervene rather than just observe when they see corruption or violence. In response to concerns about democratic back-sliding, the OSCE has begun to send monitors to countries where democracy has been long established to 'assess' rather than 'observe'.

An attempt to secure an election can also be a double-edged sword. In May 2023, voters in England had to show identity documents for the first time to be able to cast a ballot. The government argued the new measure matched international precedent; their opponents accused them of voter suppression. Early analysis by the UK Electoral Commission showed that 0.7 per cent of people were turned away but that two-thirds returned with their documents later that day, leaving 14,000 unable to vote. The conversation was complicated by the fact that older people could show the cards that gave them free bus travel (because these required an ID check to receive), whereas younger people could not (because theirs were handed out without an ID check).

The condensed idea
Democracy defended

47 Long-termism and effective altruism

I n 1790, the Irish political thinker Edmund Burke wrote: 'Society is indeed a contract . . . it becomes a partnership not only between those who are living, but between those who are living, those who are dead, and those who are to be born'. Ever since, his words have been used by conservatives to argue that future generations should be taken into account when making decisions today. Think of centre-right politicians when they warn about the burden placed on your children and grandchildren by having to repay government debt (an interpretation of the public finances that is not universally accepted).

The idea of giving a voice to 'those who are yet to be born' has received a significant modern upgrade from the Scottish philosopher William MacAskill. An Oxford academic, MacAskill is the leading figure in the movement of 'long-termism'. He set out his thinking in his book *What We Owe the Future*, published in 2022. His basic premise is that humanity is still in its early stages and that the number of people who are going to live in the future is enormous. MacAskill calculates that if humanity exists for another million years (the average lifespan of a mammal species) and the population stays at roughly the same level, then another eighty *trillion* people will be born, outnumbering individuals alive now by 10,000 to one. But these future people cannot tweet, write articles or lobby; nor can they have influence in politics and the market. So how can their interests be represented?

MacAskill proposes a framework for judging modern-day actions that combines the significance of their impact, how long-lasting they are and whether the outcome would have happened anyway, which he calls 'contingency'. Decarbonizing the economy to halt climate change is 'the proof of concept of long-termism', he wrote. He acknowledges that people tend to prioritize the needs of those emotionally and geographically closest to them, and that the equation is one-sided because the unborn cannot help those alive today. So, he argues, the needs of the present and future should be balanced. His ultimate goal is 'eutopia' – a good world – rather than 'utopia' – a perfect world. The Scottish philosopher donates 10 per cent of his income to good causes every year, as part of an organization called Giving What We Can, which encourages others to do the same.

Long-termism is a challenge to the philosophical and accounting practice of 'discounting', where the value of decisions to future generations is reduced relative to the benefits experienced by the people living at the time.

Philanthropic origins

The origins of long-termism lie in another fairly modern movement – effective altruism (EA). It began when entrepreneurs who made their money from tech and financial services wanted to apply the techniques that made them their fortunes in their businesses to their philanthropy. This meant inventing new techniques to calculate which charitable donations would generate the most bang for their buck, treating charity like an investment in a start-up. It was a modern take on the 18th-century theory of utilitarianism proposed by the English philosopher Jeremy Bentham, who argued the correct decision was the one that benefited the most people.

An example is the philanthropic strategy of Holden Karnofsky, founder of Open Philanthropy, an organization that advises on charitable giving. His portfolio is based on a technique that he calls 'worldview diversification'. Because some people believe strongly that it is better to invest in the health of children in the developing world and others believe equally strongly that it is better to invest in animal welfare, then why not accept that both worldviews have a chance of being correct and invest in both? This spread-betting on good causes might involve losses but also increases the chances of a success, which Karnofsky calls a 'hit'.

Effective altruism took a hit in 2022 when the crypto-currency millionaire and EA advocate Sam Bankman-Fried was accused of fraud. Many of the philosophical stars of the movement have denied any involvement and point out that the EA movement is just that – a decentralized movement, not an organization with a CEO or staff.

Catastrophic risks

Related to long-termism is the study on catastrophic or existential risks. These are events such as asteroid impacts, global wars, epidemics or an 'unaligned' artificial intelligence, which could destroy the potential of the human species. Initially popularized in the early 2000s by the philosopher Nick Bostrom, the concept has been developed by British ethicist Toby Ord and others. In his book *The Precipice*, Ord calculates that the risk of humanity being severely limited in the next hundred years by an asteroid strike is one in a million. There is a 1 in 1,000 chance it could happen because of a nuclear war; a 1 in 30 chance of an engineered pandemic; a 1 in 10 chance that a malicious artificial intelligence could severely dent humanity's future. Ord concluded that, in the 20th century, the chance of a civilizational collapse was around 1 in 100. His calculation for the same outcome this century is 1 in 6, which he points out is the same odds as Russian roulette. The odds get worse with every new potentially destructive technology that is created.

Ord's strategy for managing the risks is that humanity first establishes permanent 'existential security' through international cooperation and policies for the responsible deployment of technologies such as bioengineering. (In 2020 when the book was published this seemed like theory; in 2023 it became real as world leaders began wondering how to regulate artificial intelligence after it made quick – and very public – leaps forward.) Next, Ord proposes the 'long reflection' – a period in which society thinks deeply about its future, including whether human beings could be upgraded using technology.

A world government?

A world-wide government has been proposed as a solution to planet-sized problems by figures as varied as the Italian poet Dante, the German philosopher Immanuel Kant and the physicist Albert Einstein. Visions of global governance have ranged from the Holy Roman Empire to the Communist International proposed by Marx and Engels, Woodrow Wilson's failed League of Nations, or the 'New World Order' or 'the Great Reset' perceived by conspiracy theorists. The idea that everyone is a member of a global village is the basis of the philosophical movement of cosmopolitanism – from the Greek word *kosmopolitēs*, meaning 'citizen of the world'. An extreme cosmopolitan take on immigration would reject the idea of national borders, for example. A more moderate view would be that countries should be more generous to refugees. In reality, existing global governance is a mixture of institutions (the International Criminal

Court, the International Atomic Energy Agency), international treaties (the United Nations Convention on the Law of the Seas), and general respect for the rule of law (sometimes more noticeable in the breach than the observance). Foreign policy thinkers such as the former director of Policy Planning at the US State Department Anne-Marie Slaughter have described this as the 'networked' world.

Criticisms

In 2021 a paper questioning how the study of existential risks was developing was written by Carla Cremer and Luke Kemp, researchers at Oxford and Cambridge universities. They feared that the possible risks and potential mitigations being discussed had been skewed because the field was dominated by a certain type of person (young white men). They also worried that this area of study had too much 'TUA' – a 'techno-utopian approach'. They argued that this favoured speculative technologies and made big assumptions, particularly about the number of future humans who could live on other planets if interstellar travel could be invented.

The condensed idea
A new focus on the future

48 Non-state Actors

The idea of 'non-state actors' came from foreign relations, with scholars looking for ways to analyse the influence of units that had power but not borders – terrorist groups, non-governmental organizations and multinational companies. Initially the division was between IGOs (international governmental organizations) and INGOs (international non-governmental organizations) but the term now covers a broader spectrum. To some this makes it vague and of limited usefulness, but it is a helpful way to think about the growing cast of characters in a modern democracy.

Billionaires

With wealth, comes power. *Forbes* magazine and the news agency Bloomberg disagree about ranking and worth but do agree that the world's richest people are Elon Musk (Tesla), Bernard Arnault (luxury goods), Jeff Bezos (Amazon), Larry Ellison (software), and that they each possess more than US$100 billion. They use their wealth in different ways, either by buying a social media company or a newspaper or lobbying in the ways businesspeople do.

The person who acts most like a state – at least when it comes to spending money on policies – is Microsoft founder Bill Gates, who established the Bill & Melinda Gates Foundation with his former wife. It spent US$7 billion in 2022 on fighting polio, providing immunizations and developing agriculture and other projects, according to its annual report. This is more than the foreign aid budget of Italy or Norway or Sweden. But the biggest countries can still afford to outspend the Gateses. According to the official measure of Overseas Development Assistance (ODA) provided in the same year, the US spent US$55.3 billion, Germany US$35 billion, the European Union US$23 billion and Japan US$17.5 billion.

None of today's billionaires are as rich as some of the richest influencers in history. In the 15th and 16th centuries, the mine owner, merchant and banker Jakob Fugger was probably worth more than US$400 billion, adjusted for inflation. He used his fortune to fund the election of Charles V as Holy Roman Emperor and to convince the Church to allow Christians to charge interest on loans, which revolutionized banking. He also created one of the world's first social housing programmes, a settlement called the Fuggerei.

Central bankers

Central bankers oversee trillions of dollars and their interest rate decisions are felt directly in citizens' wallets. The trend after the Second World War was to make central banks independent of politicians so that money matters were stabilized rather than politicized. Democratic oversight was provided by finance ministers and legislatures appointing the bosses and giving them targets – such as limiting inflation to 2 per cent a year (in the United Kingdom, Japan and the Eurozone) or 'maximum employment, stable prices and moderate long-term interest rates' in the case of the US Federal Reserve, the Fed.

But the central banks have been accused of failing to foresee the huge rise in inflation following the Covid pandemic and the war in Ukraine – or, predicting it would only be temporary. 'Probably one of the biggest forecast errors made since the 1970s,' according to the former chief economist of the European Central Bank, Otmar Issing. And the usual recipe of cooling down the economy by increasing the cost of borrowing collided with a cost of living crisis that had already left people feeling poorer. Yet no one gets to elect the Fed chairman, and the Bank of England governor only has to write a letter if the bank misses its inflation target.

Criticism of the central banks is nothing new, though. Quantitative easing, their tricksy policy of creating more money during the financial crisis and Covid were blamed for increasing the value of certain assets, such as houses, at the expense of people who were asset poor. Brexit supporters criticized the governor of the Bank of England for making predictions about the economic effect of the United Kingdom's departure from the EU that proved to be too gloomy. In the United States a group of senators, including Democratic and Republican candidates for president, supported legislation for greater control over the Fed. On the other hand, economist Willem Buiter accused central bankers of too often wading into political debates and told them to 'stick to their knitting', a banking phrase from the 1920s. Ed Balls, the author of the plan to grant independence to the United Kingdom's central bank in the 1990s, has called for a more 'nuanced approach' to the relationship between central bankers and governments. An increasing number of central banks have opted for transparency, publishing the minutes of the meetings where they agree interest rates.

Statutory bodies

'Under these new conditions, democracy means much more than elections. Within and outside states, independent and toothy watchdog bodies have begun to reshape the landscapes of power.' This was the definition of 'monitory democracy', developed by the founder of the London Centre for Democracy, John Keane. By this he meant that societies were developing new institutions to hold power to account, beyond the traditions of liberal, representative democracy.

As an example, he gave South Africa's Truth and Reconciliation Commission (TRC). This was formed in 1995 to decide who should be eligible for an amnesty for the 'trigger pullers' of the racial struggle that was agreed during negotiations between Nelson Mandela and the outgoing apartheid government. It received 22,000 statements from people who had suffered 'torture, killings, disappearances and abductions, and severe ill treatment suffered at the hands of the apartheid state' – the human rights abuses specified in the legislation that established the TRC. Despite criticisms that it did not reveal the full truth and that many people escaped justice, the commission has been held up as a model for other countries coming to terms with conflict.

Another example of a body that could be described as part of Keane's monitory democracy is the United Kingdom's Climate Change Committee (CCC). This was set up by Britain's 2008 Climate Change Act. Every year the CCC publishes a comprehensive assessment of the government's progress against its climate targets, and whether the country is on course to hit its future 'carbon budgets' – the legally mandated limits to the emissions of greenhouse gases. The publication of the annual report is a big media moment and the most recent chair, a Conservative member of the House of Lords, was enthusiastic in his criticism of his own government. In the United Kingdom, the CCC's cousin is the Office for Budget Responsibility (OBR), whose unvarnished take on the public finances is often read more eagerly than the official statement from the government, the budget, alongside which it is published.

Think, too, of the Equalities and Human Rights Commission (EHRC), an independent body that has even found itself issuing a harsh judgment against a political party, when it investigated anti-Semitism within the opposition Labour party. But, like those powerful central bankers, democratic oversight of these organizations is weaker than over the government. Who monitors the monitors?

The condensed idea
Outside politics, but still political

49 Social Media

Ten days before the 2015 British general election, Facebook issued a jokey press release linking users' political affiliations with their cultural likes. Labour voters were fans of rock bands and one of their favourite films was *Pulp Fiction*. Conservative voters preferred pop and the spoof spy movie *Johnny English*. Liberal Democrats loved *Lord of the Rings*. Naturally, Scottish nationalists opted for *Braveheart*, the story of William Wallace's battle against the English in the 13th century. Everyone seemed to be a fan of the singer Katy Perry.

In retrospect this seems quaint and very naive. Since then, the story of social media's effect on democracy has frequently been told as a bad one. It has created 'filter bubbles' – online echo chambers where users only hear their own prejudices repeated back to them. It allows misinformation to flourish and encourages 'pile-ons' of people with unfashionable opinions. It incentivizes journalists to write stories for clicks or to fire off posts without checking the facts. And it has given the world a malign new type of business: the troll farm, described by Facebook as 'a physical location where a collective of operators share computers and phones to jointly manage a pool of fake accounts as part of an influence operation'.

Even a moment during which social media appeared to play a crucial role in promoting democracy – the Arab Spring uprising that began in 2010 and was dubbed the 'Facebook Revolution' – has been re-evaluated, with researchers suggesting other factors were more important and commentators questioning whether technology was more effectively used as a tool of oppression.

The good . . .

But there is a twist. A majority of people think social media has been a good thing for democracy, according to research carried out in 19 advanced democracies by the Pew Research Center in 2022. The top benefit attributed to social media was its power to increase awareness of issues. Respondents also said it was an effective tool to change people's minds, for drawing the attention of elected representatives to new problems and of influencing the political process overall.

The bad . . .

The country that stands out in the Pew research is the United States, where the results were flipped and 64 per cent said social media has been bad for democracy. There are plenty of reasons why Americans might feel this way.

From 2017 until 2021 the country was governed by tweet. During his presidency, Donald Trump sent 25,000 of them – an average of 18 tweets per day – to his 80 million followers. Even the existence of his account became a major political controversy. Shortly after the 6 January protests at the Capitol, in the wake of Trump's election defeat in 2020, Twitter announced that he had been banned on the basis of two tweets sent on 8 January. The platform said he had breached its rules on the incitement of violence. Then the billionaire Elon Musk bought the company and held a poll asking users whether Trump should be reinstated. Fifty-two per cent said yes and the former president was invited back. One of the reasons Musk gave for buying Twitter was that it had become biased against right-wing opinions. This accusation may help to explain why Republican voters have a more negative view of social media than Democrats.

The United States was also the target of a Russian-led 'social media campaign designed to provoke and amplify political and social discord' before and during the 2016 presidential election. That was the conclusion in 2019 of the investigation by the former director of the FBI, Robert Mueller. He found that Russia's Internet Research Agency, funded by the Russian warlord Yevgeny Prigozhin, had established Facebook groups with names such as 'Secured Borders' and 'Being Patriotic' that had reached 126 million people, and posted tweets that were seen by more than a million. These purported to be from American grassroots political associations, mostly favourable towards Donald Trump, and used material gathered on trips to the United States by Russian agents.

But perhaps American views of social media are really about something else. The number of people who told the Pew researchers that they had a negative view of social media was almost exactly the same as the number of people who said they were unhappy with the state of American democracy overall. So perhaps social media is the symptom of dissatisfaction with the political system, and not the cause?

Digital ads

Whether it is considered good, bad or ugly, social media advertising has become a major part of political campaigns. The transparency campaigners OpenSecrets estimate that US$2.1 billion has been spent on 14 million digital adverts in the United States since 2018. More than half of advertising spending on the British general election of 2019 went on online ads. From November 2023, British campaigners have to include the same official information on digital adverts as on physical leaflets.

The EU has brought in new laws restricting adverts aimed at small groups of people based on very specific characteristics in response to concerns about 'micro-targeting'. Some social media platforms have created libraries of political adverts to break down the silos that mean social media users cannot see what others are seeing, and in an attempt to provide reassurance about so-called 'dark ads', which are seen by only a few people and are not widely visible.

The condensed idea
Anti-social media?

50 Fake News

'**M**isinformation' is the umbrella term for information that is wrong. 'Disinformation' refers to false claims spread deliberately. Both have been referred to as 'fake news'. More specifically, this label applies to content that is false but designed to look genuine, for example by branding it with the logo of a reputable news organization. The cry of 'fake news' has been shouted by politicians – Donald Trump in particular – in response to stories they have not liked.

Old and new fake news

Ironically, the famous quotation about fake news by the American author Mark Twain – that 'A lie can get halfway around the world before the truth can get its boots on' – is likely to be . . . fake news. The author and founder of the Quote Investigator website Gregory Sullivan concluded that Twain probably never said it and that the phrase originated with the satirist Jonathan Swift, who wrote in 1710: 'Falsehood flies, and the Truth comes limping after it'. The phrase has been misattributed to multiple others, including Winston Churchill.

Roman emperors printed misinformation on coins. The Dreyfus Affair, the trial of an army captain that rocked France at the turn of the 20th century, was based on a forged document. The 1924 British general election hinged on a letter accusing the Labour Party of collusion with Russia that was revealed to be a fake. But social media means that modern misinformation can be produced quickly and cheaply, and passed on to billions of users. According to the World Health Organization, the claims and counter-claims about the origins of Covid, the efficacy of facemasks and the safety of vaccines meant that the pandemic was accompanied by an 'infodemic'. In 2020, the Internet Institute at Oxford University said that 81 countries employed 'cybertroops' and their main weapon was the spread of disinformation.

The psychology of information

An army of scientists is studying what happens when the brain processes information, whether true or false. They use experiments such as the cognitive reflection test (CRT), which asks questions such as: 'If a bat and ball together cost $1.10 and the bat costs $1 more than the ball, then how much does the ball cost?'

Different schools of thought emphasize different factors that contribute to the spread of misinformation. Messages that chime with a person's existing biases seem to stick. But lazy thinking might be just as powerful as biased thinking. Emotional content engages best and a person's emotional state at the time has an influence, too. Information that is familiar or coherent feels believable.

#StopTheSteal

The structures that encouraged the spread of misinformation during the 2020 US presidential election were laid out in 'The Long Fuse', an in-depth report published in 2021 by the Election Integrity Partnership, a consortium led by Stanford University. Researchers concluded that false claims were both bottom up and top down, spread by individual social media users posting claims about perceived irregularities in voting and by 'blue-check' big names such as members of the Trump family. The big social media companies had policies for tackling disinformation but these varied by platform, and were not always applied thoroughly. Then there was the rise of niche social media networks, which took a much looser approach to moderating content. Posters exploited the differences between them all. Blocking users or labelling content as malicious contributed to the feeling that free speech was being suppressed, reinforcing the narrative. It coalesced around the hashtag StopTheSteal and culminated in the 6 January protests at the Capitol.

Tackling misinformation

Responding to misinformation has become a big industry. There are at least three approaches:

De-bunking Fact-checking or issuing corrections is the classic technique to address fake news. This rests on the 'information deficit' theory that busy people make snap judgments, so just need more facts to reach more accurate conclusions. Fact-checking experts recommend that detailed alternative explanations are provided by trusted sources, with empathy for the recipients so that they do not feel patronized. Some experiments have suggested that there are limits to this method because so many other factors influence how people reach conclusions or that new facts do not automatically lead to new opinions, leading some people to recommend an alternative . . .

Pre-bunking Using the immune system as a metaphor, this is the idea that citizens can receive education and tools that act like antibodies to innoculate them against fake news. Researchers at Harvard University, for instance, created a game called Bad News which allowed players to create misinformation. Experiments suggests users became better at spotting real bad news online as a result. This concept is based on the 'growth model' view of the brain, which suggests that people like learning new skills, such as riding a bike. It is also known as 'boosting'.

System design This focuses on the changes that can be made to the functioning of the platforms, either to reduce the spread of misinformation or to warn users about it. Examples of the former include limits on the number of times a WhatsApp message can be forwarded or Twitter prompting people to read an article before retweeting it, which introduces friction into the process of sharing information. The latter includes labelling claims as false or providing links to reliable sources of information. However, there is a danger with this because studies have shown that readers then tend to believe anything that does not come with advice, known as the 'implied truth effect'.

And if a bat and ball cost $1.10 and the bat is $1 more expensive, then the ball costs $0.05.

The condensed idea
The battle for truth

Glossary

Aristocracy A description of any group at the top of society. If its privileges are passed down the generations, it is 'hereditary'.

Astroturfing Creating an apparent groundswell of public opinion to influence a debate, often using groups to make noise and post on social media. So-called because it constructs the illusion of enthusiasm coming from the grassroots.

Autocracy From the Greek *auto* ('self') and *kratos* ('power'), absolute rule focused on a single individual, who is usually not democratically elected; catch-all term for a regime with limited freedoms.

Black Lives Matter Organization set up in the US in 2013 to 'eradicate white supremacy and build local power to intervene in violence inflicted on Black communities by the state and vigilantes'; came to global prominence after the murder of George Floyd by police in 2020.

Bourgeoisie In the Marxist critique of capitalism, the property-possessing classes who also own the means of production, which gives them power over the working classes.

Commonwealth A loose political association made up of 56 countries, led by the British monarch and mainly comprising former British colonies.

Confederation A collection of self-governing territories, linked more loosely than if they were in a federation which has more formal structures for the sharing of power.

COP Annual meetings of signatories to the global agreement to reduce emissions of the gases responsible for global warming, the United Nations Framework Convention on Climate Change (UNFCCC) agreed in Rio in 1992.

Despotism Rule by an individual.

Dictatorship Rule by a leader who governs in a way that allows no dissent – e.g., Hitler, Stalin and Mussolini.

Disenfranchisement The removal or prevention of the right or ability to vote.

Faction A group that competes for power, the prevention of which was the reason the US Constitution spread authority among so many different institutions.

Fascism Ideology based on a combination of national pride, fear of national decline, ideas of racial purity and strength of an individual leader.

Federalism Processes and structures that allow power to be shared between constituent units of a country or political body.

Feudalism Modern term for the political system in medieval Europe where landowners provided security and property to tenants in return for labour. Landowners in turn pledged allegiance to a monarch and provided soldiers for their army.

First-past-the-post election Where the winner is the candidate that receives the most votes in an electoral district, which may not be greater than half of the votes – i.e., a true majority. Used for the UK Parliament and in some former British colonies.

Franchise The right to vote. New Zealand enfranchised women for parliamentary elections in 1893 – the first country to do so.

Human rights The idea that all human beings are entitled to the same, minimum guarantees. The 1948 United Nations Declaration on Human Rights includes the right to life and freedom from torture or slavery but is non-binding.

Impeachment The process of accusing a holder of office of wrong-doing.

Judicial review The power of the courts to assess the legality or constitutionality of decisions made by public bodies, for example new laws passed by legislatures.

Lobbying Seeking to steer decisions of public interest.

Mandate The power granted to a government or individual as a result of the democratic process, such as an election or referendum. Often political parties say the inclusion of a policy in their manifesto at the election gives them a mandate to deliver it.

Meritocracy A society in which status is based on ability and talent.

Nationalism A political view that accentuates membership of a nation, which may be different from the state and can lead to calls for separation or differential treatment.

Occupy Wall Street Anti-capitalist protest movement that occupied Zuccotti Park in New York's financial district between September and November 2011 and spread to other cities around the world; used the slogan: 'We are the 99%' to highlight inequalities of wealth.

Oligarchy Leadership by the few but in their own interests, rather than by a group for the good of society. Used to describe a regime where the wealthy have an undue influence over politics.

Plebiscite Another word for referendum. Based on the Latin word *plebs* meaning 'the general population'. In Australia, refers specifically to a vote that does not alter the constitution, such as the decisions in 1916 and 1917 over whether to allow conscription to the military.

Populism Political technique that leverages the opinions of 'the public' against those of 'the elite', often accompanied with disdain for the checks and balances used in a democratic system.

Proportional representation Voting system in which the outcome reflects the share of votes rather than the winner taking all. Can apply at the level of the individual electoral district or to the entire system.

Quango A quasi-autonomous non-governmental organization, especially in the UK. A body with official powers that receives public funding and is not directly controlled by ministers but is accountable to them.

Referendum When the public expresses an opinion on an issue by voting on a number of options that can be advisory or binding on the government.

Secularism A policy of placing limits on the influence of the church or religious groups on political decisions and in national life, such as preventing the 'conspicuous' display of religious symbols.

Separation of powers The division of authority between institutions so that none can dominate the others, usually between the executive, legislature and courts, as in the United States.

Sortition Use of a lottery to allocate public roles to citizens by random chance in ancient Athens. Used today to select juries in many legal systems. Advocated by some campaigners as an alternative to representative democracy.

Sovereignty In international legal terms, a country's control over territory. More broadly, the exercise of ultimate power.

Suffrage The right to vote. Sometimes separated into active suffrage (the right to vote) and passive (the right to stand as a candidate).

Tactical voting When a voter chooses a candidate they may not necessarily like to prevent the victory of a candidate they definitely dislike.

Totalitarianism A regime in which the leader seeks total control of national life, including personal relationships and even individual thought.

Tyranny of the majority Popularized by de Tocqueville and John Stuart Mill, the ability of a majority to prevail over a minority, which could have negative consequences for the latter; the reason democracies have checks and balances and minorities are protected.

Universal Basic Income A no-strings-attached payment from the state that is given to every citizen to ensure a basic level of wealth for the entire population irrespective of their employment status.

Veto The official power to stop something. The US president can veto a piece of legislation but Congress can override this with a two-thirds majority, for example.

Welfare state A governing system that caters for the wellbeing of its citizens – for example, through healthcare or cash transfers to cover periods of unemployment. Associated with the British official William Beveridge who, in the 1940s, called on the state to eliminate the 'five giants' of want, disease, ignorance, squalor and idleness.

Index

About the author

Adam Fleming presents the BBC's daily podcast *Newscast* and Radio 4's *AntiSocial*. Previously, he was the Chief Political Correspondent and covered the Brexit negotiations as Brussels Correspondent. His first job in journalism was on the children's programme *Newsround*.

Greenfinch,
An imprint of Quercus Editions Ltd
Carmelite House
50 Victoria Embankment
London EC4Y 0DZ
An Hachette UK company

First published in 2023

A CIP catalogue record for this book is available from the British Library

PB ISBN 9781529434170
eBook ISBN 9781529434194

10 9 8 7 6 5 4 3 2 1

Printed and bound in Great Britain by Clays Ltd, Elcograf S.p.A.

Papers used by Greenfinch are from well-managed forests and other responsible sources.